TWELVE INCHES

BRIDGING THE GAP BETWEEN
WHAT YOU KNOW ABOUT GOD AND HOW YOU FEEL

BY

PATRICIA HOLBROOK

*He designed you
to SOAR!*

Patricia Holbrook

Comfort PUBLISHING

Isa 40:31

TWELVE INCHES

For information, address Comfort Publishing, 296 Church St. N., Concord, NC 28025. The views expressed in this book are not necessarily those of the publisher.

First printing

Book cover design by Reed Karriker

ISBN: 978-1-938388-49-1
Published by Comfort Publishing, LLC
www.comfortpublishing.com

Printed in the United States of America

Table of Contents

To Steve, life is so much better with you.
I love you more

Foreword

Most of us can remember a time in our childhood, even if surrounded by poverty or family dysfunction, when we truly believed that we held the world on a string and that unlimited opportunities to write our own story were but a flick of the wrist away. Our imaginations had no ceiling and that little piece of *Annie* in all of us was certain that the sun was really coming out tomorrow.

For some, that naive and serene bubble managed to hold first chair in the symphony of our lives well into adulthood — in some cases, long enough to cause us to think we were the master conductor of our destiny, able to choreograph a life-melody free of ditches, disease, dead-ends, disappointments, deception and out-right diabolical darkness. Yet, sooner or later we come to realize that this narrative called life is much bigger than just our part.

When knocked down, pushed aside, kicked back or even just flat-out run over by circumstances beyond our control, by the misdeeds of others and/or those of our own choosing, we long for our "lane", our "rightful place", our walk of fame instead of our hall of shame. We crave for separation from whatever holds us back.

If you have ever been there ... you know, in that parallel universe, feeling blown way off course, confused, bewildered, overwhelmed, left with far more questions than answers while full of uncertainty about God and His purposes, Twelve Inches is indeed just for you. Consider this book as an invitation from the extraordinary Patricia

Holbrook to get small for a time, to descend to a much lower elevation and find the counter-winds of heaven which are able to reverse your course, blow fresh hope into your life and guide you into a never-before experienced embrace in the arms of our all-loving Heavenly Father.

Perhaps you have told yourself for years that something is missing — perhaps your efforts to get close to God by being busy in and around church and religion have only left you feeling farther from His presence than ever before. If honest, your soul would admit in these moments that you desperately want to "feel alive" again — or maybe, just maybe, alive for the very first time.

Perhaps you have wrestled with these very doubts and questions — maybe they hound your soul this very day. In *Twelve Inches,* Patricia Holbrook provides a resource that not only helps us understand where and how we allow our minds to be vulnerable, risking succumbing to doubt and defeat during our seasons of testing, but she also provides a road map to finding and experiencing the life-giving and life-transforming difference between a life lived for Christ ... and a life lived in Christ ... the abundant to overflowing kind of life our Father in heaven designed for us all along.

For those who have thought about or have even dared to dip their toe into this thing called the Gospel, you would have to admit that our minds and our emotions can easily allow the injustices and perversions of this world to throw the goodness of God and the very Word of God on trial. So, fair warning: if you dare to dive into *Twelve Inches,* you will quickly find yourself saturated in a very personal and profound life reflection that flows from a soul who has been tested in every way, and has proven God's Word to be true in every trial. Patricia challenges your faith as she bares her soul with the lessons learned through her personal valleys. Her testimonies shout out from each page: God is indeed faithful and

His mercies truly endure forever.

May you be richly blessed, as the life-giving counter winds of Heaven that flow from the truths contained in this book blow fresh purpose and peace into every corner of your life.

How does it feel to know you're just 12 Inches away?

— Rev. David B. Miller

Acknowledgements

Four years ago, when God called me to start Soaring with Him Ministries, I had many doubts, fears of rejection and feelings of inadequacy. Like Moses, I knew it was God who was calling, but I certainly knew that I was completely inadequate for the task. Despite my feelings, I chose to "bridge the twelve-inch gap" and simply tell my heart to trust the God I know. The publishing of this book is nothing but a sequence of miraculous events, orchestrated by God with the purpose to bring glory to His Name and point others to His Son. I am nothing but "a jar of clay"; prove that this "all-surpassing power is from God and not from me." (2 Corinthians 4:7).

To Yahweh, the God of the Covenant and His Son, Yeshua, Messiah: Thank you for entrusting me with a small piece of the Kingdom. I give You all the glory.

When God chooses us to be the recipients of His beautiful gifts, He rejoices in using people in our lives to bring the gifts to fruition. I certainly would not have finished the first page, were it not for a multitude of people cheering me on along the way.

To My amazing husband Steve — You are God's greatest gift to me. You believed in me when I didn't believe in myself. You cheered me on when I was discouraged; you nursed me when I was sick. You make me laugh, and that is priceless. You're the biggest example in my life of someone who has a strong Twelve-Inch Bridge. I love you with a love that words can't describe. Let's grow old together.

To My daughters Adriana and Isabella — my very own cheer-leaders — when I was a young girl, I dreamed of having daughters. When doctors told me I couldn't conceive, I still believed. You are God's grace in flesh. You make me a better person. I love to watch you grown into beautiful young ladies, who love Jesus, family and the people around you. I can't wait to see what God will do in and through you. Thank you for sharing me with the computer, each time God puts a message in my heart. I love you!

To Mom and Dad: thank you for all the sacrifices you made and still make for me and my family. Thank you for coming to America when we can't come to Brazil. You have been the best parents a girl could have. You are both living examples of God's love and grace. Jorge: Thank you for being a wonderful step-dad for me and my family. I love each of you with all my heart.

To My sister Ana Maria and her family, and my brother Joao Guilherme: I miss you so much. I wish we still lived only a couple of hours away, as we did for many years. But we know that our hearts are always together. I love you all!

To my husband's entire family, especially my father-in-law Marion and mother-in-law Pauline. Thank you for taking me in as your own and for being there for me when I moved six thousand miles away from my family and friends. You have always loved me and I'm forever grateful for that. I love you all!

To the Soaring with Him ministry team: Terri, Bettina, Lilly, Christy, Adriana and my brother Guigo — I couldn't have asked God for a better group of people to do ministry work with. Your giving heart, prayers and support have sustained me through this journey. When I was on a tight deadline to finish this manuscript, I'd go to a coffee shop early on Saturdays and would text the group asking for prayers. I know that I couldn't have finished the manuscript on time were it not for these wonderful saints covering me with prayers. I love each of you dearly. Thank you for believing in me.

To my pastor Dr. Charles Stanley – When we joined First Baptist Church of Atlanta in 2000, I was a newly converted Christian. Through your practical teaching and encouragement from the pulpit every Sunday, you have instilled in my heart the desire to (in your own words) *obey God and leave all consequences to Him*. The publishing of this book is only one of the examples of the results obtained by applying that principle to my life. Your teaching has guided me through many storms and encouraged me to believe and fully trust God. My family and I are blessed to be under your ministry. Thank you, Pastor!"

To Pastor Rodney Brooks and his wife Michelle — When God called me into ministry, you were the first ones to believe in me. Rodney agreed to distribute my devotionals to the FBA Worship choir, making this 200 plus choir group my very first audience. Michelle invited me to speak for the first time at a choir ministry outreach. You are a true example of godly leadership.

To the Atlanta Worship Choir — You were my first audience and you have no idea of how many times your encouraging comments helped me gain new resolve to continue writing. When I went through cancer, you were there for me. You lifted me up in prayers and song. I am blessed to be part of this amazing group of people.

It's definitely more than singing! Thank you for reading and sharing my devotionals!

To Tracy Brown, AJC — Thank you for believing in my writing and giving me the chance to write a faith column in a secular major newspaper. You have been instrumental to take my message to the larger audiences. To Patty Murphy, my AJC editor — thank you for your encouragement and helpful insights! God bless you both!

To the Comfort Publishing team: Kristy, when we met at She Speaks Conference, you told me something that made my heart sing for joy. You smiled and said: "You may just be the person I came here for." You have been excited about this project from the first moment we met and I can't thank you enough for believing in my writing as you have. Lynn, thank you for editing the manuscript with such mastery and ease. Thank you for making me look better, all the while maintaining my writing style and voice. You rock! Jason and Pamela, thank you for believing in this project and betting on a first time author. Thank you for patiently answering my rookie questions. It's been a pleasure working with you all.

To Marcus and Lisa Ryan — Thank you so much for taking the time to talk to my husband and I about the ins and outs of the publishing industry. Your candid input and advice made us feel very confident to embark on this journey.

To my friends and endorsers: Amy Carroll from Proverbs 31 Ministries, Audra Haney from the 700 Club, Eleni Leite from Precepts Ministry International, George Saffo from iDisciple, Rev. David Miller from Life Letter Café, Carol Smith from Operation Christmas Child, Yvonne Conte from Day of Joy Ministries, author Kimberly Rae,

TV host and author Lisa Ryan, Pastor Jim Haines from First Baptist Dallas, Pastor Rodney Brooks and Mary Gellersted, both from First Baptist Atlanta — Thank you all for taking the time to read my manuscript and for endorsing the message therein. Each of you has touched my life in a special way. May God bless you greatly!

And finally — There's a friend that sticks closer than a brother. I would like to take a minute to thank my closest friends in this world, people who have been there for me and my family in more ways than we can count. Some of you have been a vital support of my ministry since its inception, encouraging me with each small victory. Others have simply been there for my family through thick and thin, making it a bit easier for me to keep the faith through life's trials. I love you dearly for loving me: Adriana and Julio Valgas, Terri and Price Potter, Robin and Keidra McKibben, Bettina and Mike Rann, Connie and Jerry Allen, Stephanie and Joey Wilkins, Chasity and Dave Dedman, Shary and Rog Dyer, Sandra and Erol Onal.

Endorsements

"Although I've been a passionate follower and student of Jesus for over 35 years, I often find myself in the tension between what I say I believe and how I live. In *Twelve Inches,* Patricia Holbrook takes us on a journey to bridge that gap with deep faith. Step by step she walks us over the bridge toward a destination of abundant life in Jesus. I've finished Patricia's book with my hands full of the tools I need to live a greater faith!"

— Amy Carroll, Proverbs 31 Ministries Speaker and Writer, Author of *Breaking Up with Perfect*

"*Twelve Inches* felt less like a book and more like a conversation with a faithful friend. Full of transparency, vulnerability, and faithfulness to the truth of God — this powerful book hit home in so many ways. Patricia's words comfort and challenge, reveal and refocus, humble and help. This work is a beautiful gift to the body of Christ and I cannot recommend it enough."

— Audra Haney, Writer/Producer for the 700 Club

"I greatly enjoyed this extremely thought-provoking book that leads to the answer of a very important question: How can I develop a deep and meaningful relationship with God, beyond a mere intellectual knowledge of Him? How can I keep on believing when troubles strike and my emotions get on the way of great faith? I believe this book contains the Biblical principles that, if applied, have the power to transform hearts and minds and encourage many to serve Him wholeheartedly. I highly recommend it!"

—Eleni Leite, Precept Ministries International,
Portuguese Speaking Countries Director

"Patricia Holbrook's book *Twelve Inches* has truly awakened me spiritually and reminded me that being God's child is about more than going to church and being a good person. Her personal testimonies and candor bring reality to the pages, making her teachings very relevant. I will be sure to stay focused on Jesus in all I do, and in difficult times tell my heart what I know about God: He is my Healer, Deliverer, Constant Friend and Savior. Thank you, Patricia for following the leading of God's Spirit to write this book. It will be a blessing to all who read it!"

— George Saffo, Content Acquisition Manager, iDisciple, LLC

"*Twelve Inches* is an eye opening reminder of God's infinite love for His children. With complete honesty, Patricia has allowed her readers to realize the unfiltered truth behind our disconnection with the Father and all that He desires for us. She has remarkably captured in her own life's experience the essence of building the "Twelve-inch Faith Bridge" and a compelling challenge for us to do the same! Beautifully written, it is a book that every Believer should read and share with a lost friend or loved one."

— Rodney Brooks, Minister of Music,
First Baptist Church of Atlanta

Loneliness. Loss. Cancer. Patricia Holbrook has been through enough personal trials to know what it feels like to wonder what God is up to, even sometimes doubting his goodness. *Twelve Inches* is a book about trusting God, even through life's darkest trials, on the road to experiencing the truth of God's immeasurable love regardless of your circumstances.

— Carol Smith, Area Coordinator, Operation Christmas Child

"For every woman who feels defeated, stressed, insecure, or just weary of wanting an abundant life but not finding it, read this book! I was blessed by it, learned from it, and plan to keep a copy in my resource library to read and reference in the future — both personally and for ministry."

— Kimberly Rae, award-winning author of 20 books

"The distance may be short but the journey can take a lifetime. In *Twelve Inches*, Patricia bridges the gap between your emotions and what you know about God. This book will help you begin to walk in the spiritual reality and maturity you long for. Patricia shares her own journey in a way that will help you live your life as a vibrant Christian. You'll discover, twelve inches is all it takes to love the Lord with all your heart and with all your mind."

— Lisa Ryan, Christian TV Host, author, speaker

"Patricia has given us a great tool to help us understand the difference between how we feel and what we know to be true. This is an easy read with real life stories and examples of how God has worked in her life and how He can work in yours."

— Yvonne Conte, Day of Joy Ministries, Fort Myers, FL

"In a knowledgeable and loving manner, *Twelve Inches* helps us better understand our personal faith in God, while compelling us to build our Twelve-inch brain-to-heart bridge in order to prevent our emotions from guiding our destiny. It's an insightful and helpful resource to help us learn that God has so much more for us than what we have experienced.

As Patricia helps us understand how to "bridge the gap between how we feel and what we know about God", we are reminded that God has the power to redo and remake us in a unique way. The society in which we live needs to hear this. A very important read."

— Mary Gellerstedt, Director, Global Missions,
First Baptist Church of Atlanta

I have known Patricia and Steve for many years. They are the real deal and I am blessed to count them as friends. You owe it to yourself to read the book and to learn from Patricia's experience with trials, temptation, testing and trusting the Lord. The counsel she provides in this book is biblical and born out of personal experience. Read the book, have her speak for your event, get to know her and get to know Him better!

— Pastor Jim Haines, Minister to Boomers and Seniors
First Baptist Dallas

Introduction

I was sitting at our dining room table, pregnant with our younger daughter, slowly going through the motions of the day. The cup of decaf coffee set on the table, untouched. Before me, I had my Bible open to a page which showed highlighted marks and much rereading of the same passage. Just days before, I had decided to study once again the Gospel of John. The dear apostle's love story about the Savior has long been one of my favorites . I was feeling a bit lost, in a spiritual desert, questioning God about the past months' events. A failing business which caused a great financial stress headed an ever-growing list of complaints that I had been bringing to God every day in prayer.

I was on the tenth chapter of John when I read the verse that would propel me into a new phase of my spiritual walk. This verse was there, highlighted and underlined, proof that it had been studied several times before. But that day, John 10:10 jumped out of the page to embrace my heart:

"I came that they may have life, and have it abundantly."

I sat there for a minute, drinking it in.

Abundant life?! "I am not living an abundant life!" I admitted to myself. Maybe overly hectic and certainly full, but not the kind of abundance of which Jesus spoke. Not at all.

While meditating on Jesus' words, a sober realization filled my soul. I was going through the motions of religion: attending church, reading the Bible and saying my prayers. But deep down inside, I felt empty and, well, unfulfilled. My faith was shallow and my walk was frail. No, life was not abundant at all. The realization of my fragile spirituality made me genuinely sad. My fluctuating pregnancy hormones helped me admit that I could benefit from a good cry. However, more than anything else, I realized that I wanted more. The very abundant life that Christ promised, that's what I wanted. A rock-solid faith, one that saw beyond one's circumstances, that's what I needed. Yes, I wanted what Jesus promised and I became determined to find it!

I found out that I was not alone. According to a Barna Group survey from 2006,[1] fourty-five percent of Americans are professed born-again Christians. If that is true, how can we explain the state our society is in today? If more Christians lived from Monday through Saturday the lives that we sing about on Sunday morning, not only our nation, but our world would be a better, happier place.

Could it be that we, Christians, are losing that which made us stand out before the world almost as super heroes in the dawn of the Early Church? As John Bevere describes on his book Extraordinary:

"In Contrast to the present reputation of Christians, one of the great struggles the early church encountered was convincing people that believers were not super-heroes or gods. Cornelius, an officer in the most powerful army in the world, bowed down to worship Peter and his companions. Stunned, Peter immediately replied, "Stand Up; I myself am also a man" (Acts 10:26)"[2]

It seems as if many of us have never possessed that pivotal evidence of abundance and divine power. I firmly believe that the reason we don't is because we are missing an important faith-walk connection. And for Heaven's and our own sake, we need it. Badly. We must learn how to stun the world with our faith.

This book was born in my heart as a result of my personal spiritual journey from an apathetic and anxious Christian to a woman who is now excited about life and who has honestly found the peace that surpasses all understanding through hard trials. In the past seven years, I have been through three major surgeries, cancer, great financial loss and a tragic death in my immediate family. We've had our baby girl at the hospital twice without diagnosis from the doctors either time. These years have also been some of the most amazing, fulfilling years of my life. No, I cannot claim to have it together at all times, but I have come to understand that there is much more to this life than many of us, God's children, have been aware. Yes! Life can be beautifully abundant with Jesus, regardless of our circumstances. It's true, my friend. The problem is though, that many of us have accepted Him as our Lord and Savior and are Heaven-bound, but we often don't seem to be able to fully grasp God's grace, power and love towards us. Many of us are depressed, anxious and clueless of what to do with our lives. To this, I can attest from personal experience.

Unfortunately, I am afraid our group is not confined to the space outside our church doors. You will actually find us saying powerful, moving prayers in front of our Bible study groups; you will find us lifting our hands up high in worship on Sunday mornings and even serving in different ministries within our churches. However, if you were to look inside our hearts and minds, you would probably find a disconnection between what we say is true and how we actually live, act in our lives, simply because we do not really know how to apply God's truths in our lives. Bridging the infamous twelve-inch distance (hereafter called Twelve-Inch Faith Bridge) between one's brain and one's heart is decisive when it comes to living a purposeful, spirit-filled, world-stunning life. From the newly converted Christian to seasoned pastors who fill our country's pulpits every Sunday, we Christians desperately need to connect that Twelve-Inch gap in order to have the abundant life that Christ promised.

Can you relate? Do you feel like there is a disconnection between what you say you believe and how you act out your faith? If you do, this book is for you. My prayer is that, as I share my struggles with you and the lessons I have learned from building my personal Twelve-Inch Faith Bridge, your faith will be challenged, tested and strengthened.

Now, fair warning, you will be invited to dig a little deeper and experiment with God's Word as we dare together to truly believe the Promises, Truths and Principles that He teaches us. We are going to learn not to let our hearts rule us, but rather, learn to rule our hearts. We are going to be challenged to train our hearts not to lean on our feelings, but on what we know about our God.

My purpose is that by the end of this book, you will discover a different YOU in Christ. What I found out is that He did not design us to live perched between the rocks, limited and fearful. God designed us to soar like the eagles, above anything and everything.

Come join me on this project of building your personal brain-to-heart connection: Your very own Twelve-Inch Faith Bridge. It will not be as easy as a walk in the park. You will be challenged with difficult questions — just for you — (of course, no one is listening but you and God.) You will be challenged to give up things that may be very dear to you. You will be counseled to truly believe the Word of God for what it says about your position as a child of the Maker of the universe. You will be advised to start delighting yourself in the feast that God has prepared in His Word for His people. A feast that has everything your soul needs to grow and mature in Christ and to become everything He has designed you to be from the beginning of time.

Keep in mind that I have become quite familiar with this process. I have known both the uneasy feeling of something missing when everything seems to be in place, as well as the feeling of not understanding as I watched some Christians go through the hardest valleys with a smile on their faces. I didn't know, once, what made God's people sing for joy, regardless of their circumstances. Now I know: their secret is a strong, solid connection between how they feel and what they know about their God. It is a strong Twelve-Inch Faith Bridge.

The early church Christians found the blueprint and built theirs.

Now, by the power of the Holy Spirit, let's build yours!

May I start by praying with you?

"Lord, I may not know the person who is holding this book, but You do. You have written each day of his or her life before they were even conceived. I pray that You envelope them with Your love, grace and wisdom today. May the words in this book shed some light on their path. May You use the lessons from this journey to teach us how to find the abundant life that You promised Your children through Your Son, the Christ. May You open our spiritual eyes to see the fullness of Your love, the greatness of Your power and Your amazing, all sustaining grace. We give it all to You. And to You alone be the glory, Father. In in the precious Name of Jesus I pray. Amen."

Chapter 1

When Your Mind is Starving

I looked down at my pretty white clothes and could not believe this outfit was my choice before leaving home. I knew where I was going. And yet, I chose to wear a brand new white outfit. As I looked at the junk that needed to be moved from the storage area, realization set in. My clothes would be ruined by day's end. What was I thinking?

Of course. I wasn't thinking.

One of the reasons many of us have a hard time keeping our faith when facing life's circumstances is because we allow our minds and lives to become contaminated by our environment.

We go to church on Sundays and put on a white, beautiful garment, as God's Word molds our character and attitudes. We leave refreshed and empowered to be salt and light. Our beautiful white clothes are ready to reflect godly character in the world. Then, often before Sunday is over, we allow ourselves to be tainted by the junk that the entertainment industry promotes, or waste precious time mindlessly browsing through social media walls.

The choices of what we feed our minds stain our attitude and ruin our commitment to shine. All because we choose to walk into a dumpster wearing beautiful, white garments.

"Do not be conformed to this world, but be transformed by the renewal of your mind, that by testing you may discern what is the

will of God, what is good and acceptable and perfect. "
Romans 12:2 (NASB)

In 1993, the California Milk Association Board created the beloved "Got milk?"advertisement campaign. It successfully ran until 2014 throughout the United States in broadcast and print and at this writing is still active in California. As you flipped through the pages of just about any magazine in the United States, you were likely to find an adult who was an athlete or a celebrity, whose image was connected to good health or strength, wearing a milk moustache. Designed to boost milk sales and milk consumption, it was a famous and powerful advertisement used to instill in adults the desire to drink something that is usually a child's favorite.

The smart marketers behind the campaign knew exactly what they were doing. Adults don't generally drink much milk. Children do. Adults like substance. Something they can bite into. Like meat.

Just as our bodies need proper rest and nutritious foods in order to function properly, grow stronger and remain healthy, our minds must likewise be fed daily with wholesome choices, if we expect to have a strong faith-walk connection.

The benefits we receive from feeding our minds with God's Word are irrefutable. But I would like to take one step back and reflect on other things we take in on a daily basis, whether we realize it or not. I'd like to propose that although we may digest relevant and impactful *spiritual truth* as we read our bibles, it is often neutralized by junk and empty information that is served by our environment in silver trays daily.

From TV programs to movies we watch, from the music we hear to everything Internet, we are bombarded with information that is, at best, unrealistic and unimportant. We are plugged into a world of make-believe, where our relationships look inadequate, our possessions look meager and Christianity is portrait as weak, pathetic and hypocritical.

As we plug into technology and entertainment and load our brains with its shaded views, we find ourselves too weak to make godly decisions.

And our Faith Bridge starts to crack.

This chapter intends to expose the first issue that prevents us from having a strong faith-walk connection. We certainly cannot keep on sailing the rough waters of life if our thoughts are drowned by indecision. We certainly cannot live a victorious spiritual life if our minds are starving for wholesome thoughts. There are culprits of this starvation, and my intent is to expose them in this chapter.

Culprit: The interrupting sound of technology

It seems as if my brain is on constant drive these days. My feet hit the floor in the morning and my eyes have not quite adjusted to the light before I hit the home button of my smart phone. The screen glares at me as if to say: "Take a breath, woman. I'll be here after breakfast. There are other important things in your life."

I cannot stop at a traffic light without being tempted to reach out to my phone and check if anything has changed from … uh … 30 seconds before.

It's pitiful, I admit. But judging from what I see around me, this is certainly not just my personal issue. It's an epidemic.

Dining out is an altogether new experience these days. I was at a restaurant with my family not long ago. As we settled at our table, I scanned the territory around: A group of teenagers, a young couple seemingly on a date and another couple and their 5 year-old son. They were all holding on to their thingamajigs as if the air

3

that they breathed was trapped inside the keyboards. The young couple exchanged only a couple of sentences all evening. Their best conversation seemed to be reserved to whoever was reading their social media pages or texts.

I don't mean to sound critical, much less judgmental, since I have often been guilty of the same flaws, but you don't have to be overly observant to realize that technology owns too much of our time.

Truthfully, life was already very busy before these niceties came along claiming our attention 24/7, but now it seems as if we have allowed them to rob our attention from just about anything we do. Shamefully, I heard my older daughter ask me if I was listening, because I had to grab my phone in the midst of a conversation.

Gizmo buzzed and Mom went to it. I've been treating it like a colicky baby.

Don't get me wrong; I'm not suggesting that we drive a hammer through everything we own with an LCD screen. But I think we have a growing problem in the western world. Not only is technology impersonalizing our relationships, it is also claiming the best of our minds. It is demanding our attention when we should be plugged into more important matters, such as quality time with God and family.

We're able to waste time nosing around or inflating our egos on social media walls and yet have a hard time finding fifteen minutes of quietness before our God. Social media is a wonderful way to stay connected to the people in our lives. But it cannot become more important than our connection with God. If we are to listen to what He has to say to us, we must learn to unplug. Be still, and patiently wait to hear from Him.

As interesting as social media can be, it also creates a series of other issues for the believer. We can get caught up in the dangerous trap of comparison. We see what our friends are doing, or buying, vacation trips they are taking, or their spiritually-filled posts and we become enamored with a reality that is not ours. "If only I could write like she does." "If only my husband was that sweet!" We go on comparing ourselves to others, all along forgetting that God wrote a unique story for each of us. No one has the same gifts and talents as you. No one will have the same trials or blessings. No one will have your story.

As we compare our walls to other people's, we forget that our gifts are different than theirs and we become competitive and envious, wallowing in a discontent that we brought on ourselves.

Culprit: The one-eyed monster

Now, television is an altogether separate issue. I have found myself growing weary of looking for anything worth watching among the list of over 200 channels that our satellite company provides. Some programs are merely shallow and silly. However, I always take issue with the violence, depraved sexuality and horror that I can find between channels 2 and 800. I also take issue with the fact that we have to be so careful when we turn on the TV around our children … at two o'clock in the afternoon! And yet, the truth is, a quick visit around social media sites and you will find out that many Christians are watching (and promoting) the very worst of television.

The result is that, as we continue to feed our minds with the junk that is on television, our spiritual muscles become increasingly weakened. And our minds become certainly full and yet, malnourished. The entertainment industry is selling compromise after compromise these days. We're numbed into believing that choices and lifestyles that are contrary to what the scriptures teach are acceptable.

Truthfully, the more we feast on these worldly values, the harder it is to discern truth. As we become increasingly distanced from God's Word and its principles, we start hearing statics as we try to hear from Him. Our channels of communication with the divine are jeopardized.

Culprit: Music

We don't live in the 50's anymore. As a matter of fact, we don't have to go back so far to realize how much our society has changed in the past fifty years. Music has certainly kept up with the decline of morals of our day.

I spent my entire school life in Catholic institutions. I started playing the piano at a very young age and was exposed to classic and religious tunes during my childhood. Then as a teenager in the 80's, my world spun around as I fell in love with Michael Jackson, Madonna and Tina Turner. They rocked my world and the world of music as I knew it. New moves, new clothes, new beats. And although their moves and clothes were often racy, they pale in contrast with what we see in music entertainment today.

Music videos have introduced a new, subtle level of pornography. Lyrics invite our children to live unrestrained lives. Singers curse at us and promote the demoralization of women, as well as the use of drugs.

We have seen it all. Yet many of us refuse to change radio stations.

Always plugged in

We do not have to be neuroscientists to realize that our brains are under the influence of an ever-expanding world of new, faster technology each day. It is hard to concentrate in writing this chapter without being interrupted by my computer or phone, announcing that a new email is in the inbox.

Phones interrupt our conversations. Computers remain on when we get home from work. TVs remain on while families eat dinner. We are forever plugged in. Technology is a wonderful thing and yet, when not used properly, it certainly has the potential to keep our minds so busy with worldly affairs that we find it hard to quiet down and hear God, much less listen to Him.

Spiritual ADHD is growing rampant in our modern society, as busy minds are filled with too much information, making it hard to concentrate on what God is doing in our lives or trying to tell us. We are not even talking about the truly unwholesome things that permeate our cyberspace today, such as pornography and sex chat sites.

I can't remember life without some type of cell phone, although I did not own one until I was 23. Then some years ago, we were introduced to smart phones. We can indeed efficiently conduct our lives from our fingertips these days. Yet, we have become over-plugged into the world and under-plugged into the source of our strength and wisdom. It seems hard to spend ten minutes in uninterrupted prayer, and yet one can lose himself in Internet trances for hours on end.

The result is brains that are filled with more of the cares of this world and often less of godly information that would help us live more fruitful and abundant lives.

If only God would text me!

"If we are weak in communion with God we are weak everywhere."
Charles Spurgeon

With the overflow of technology in our days, many of us are guilty of spending less time with God. I am certain that one of the biggest reasons for that is because our hyperactive minds are flooded with information that is at best unimportant.

The difference between spending quality time with God or not may just mean the difference between a purposeful life and a wasted one. That does sound harsh, but it is true

"For where your treasure is, there your heart will be also."
Matthew 6:21 (NIV)

Internal war

I woke up with a new resolution that day. I prayed before getting out of bed to start my morning routine: Read my Bible. Check. Pray. Check. Write in my journal my goals for the day. Check.

After dropping my children at school, I went for a walk and was talking to God as I basked in the beauty of nature. I felt so close to Him. I was ready to take the day by the horns and make the most of it. This day was going to matter!

I sat at my desk later that morning, ready to start writing. My mind was filled with ideas and determination to cross off several items in my to-do list for the day. Then it happened. An email came in, with information that led me to a website, then to another and another. One hour was gone before I returned to my Word file. My thoughts were scattered. My fingers could not move forward. I was stuck.

After finally getting myself focused again and writing a couple more paragraphs, my stomach reminded me it was lunch time. I made a sandwich and, since I hate to eat by myself, sat in front of the TV. My browsing took me to a station where two guys were telling the audience everything about celebrities lives. "Like I care," I thought. Instead of moving forward however, curiosity took over. My search stopped right there. Over one hour later, I shamed myself into getting off the couch and back to my desk. By then, it was about time to pick up my children from school.

My God-given to do list of four measly items had one check on it at the end of the day.

I was distracted by too much information and mystified by celebrities' glitter. Thus one wasted day ended.

I know many can relate to my experience. We have all been there. We allow our curiosity and often laziness to take over our days and waste precious, irretrievable time.

Mind over matter

"But I see in my members another law waging war against the law of my mind and making me captive to the law of sin that dwells in my members." Romans 7:23

Within this verse in Romans lies a revelation that we all must attain if we are to build a strong Twelve-Inch Faith Bridge. Truth is, our flesh is ever wrestling against what our spirit knows as true and good. The "Law of my mind" that Paul mentions in this verse is the same as the Law of the Spirit. It is the Law and perception to distinguish between right and wrong that we received as we invited Christ into our lives. It is the knowledge for which our spirit craves.

However, at the same time that our spirits crave for the things of God, our flesh craves for the things of the world. It is truly an ongoing war and it shall end only the day we die. Paul summarizes His struggles on the same chapter when He says: "For the good that I want, I do not do, but I practice the very evil that I do not want." Romans 7:19.

Who cannot relate to this truth? Who has not rehearsed a good day on their mind, good attitudes and great deeds, just to fail at their first attempt?

I'm raising my hand right now.

We cannot win this war on our own, and we certainly will not win it if we continually feed our minds rubbish.

We know the truth, however. If we don't feed our spirit properly, our bodies will always tend to go the opposite way of where God wants to lead us.

"The flesh has a passionate desire to suppress the Spirit, and the Spirit has a passionate desire to suppress the flesh. And these are set in opposition to each other so that you may not do the things which you desire to do." Galatians 5:17

Weeding out the things of the world

But what is the answer? you may ask. Should we just shut down all electronics and only listen to gospel music and watch sermons on TV?

This is a very personal choice. You should ask God to show you, if there are current activities and programs that do not fit who you are in Christ. He will show you. Even right now, you probably have something that comes to your mind. These may be television shows, music or movie selections. My purpose is not to judge your choices, but rather to remind you, that if we are to remain in Christ, we must turn off the world's values from our minds and turn away from its ways.

For several years after salvation, I lived pretty mingled with the rest of the world. I was very vocal about what I believed and tried hard to live a life of good repute. However, in actions and deeds, my life amounted very little for the kingdom of God. I would read my Bible without consistency and yet, consistently watch unwholesome programs and movies. I would nod in approval of what my pastor would say from the pulpit on Sunday and quickly forget it on Monday morning as I faced difficult circumstances and temptations.

"If the world hates you, keep in mind that it hated me first. If you belonged to the world, it would love you as its own. As it is, you do not belong to the world, but I have chosen you out of the world. "
John 15:18-19 (NASB)

Today I am certain that the reason my faith and walk were so frail was because I was insisting on living as a double-minded creature, caught between the love and allegiance to my Savior and the lures and answers of the world. I kept on trying to please a world that hated me because of my new connection with Christ.

Jesus spoke clearly to you and me in the verses above: He has chosen us and "extracted" us out of the world. We cannot continue to live a life that is entangled between pleasing God and men, searching Him and at the same time looking for worldly pleasures and still expect unshaken faith. We cannot expect to be loved by the world and please our Savior at the same time.

If we are to remain in Christ, we must choose to walk guided by a renewed mind. We cannot expect to have unshaken faith and live in purity, if we fill our minds with the junk that entertainment producers fill our TV stations and movie theaters with these days. We cannot expect to remain faithful and be the light of the world and the salt of the earth, if when we are with people who don't know God, we blend so perfectly with the crowd that we cannot be told apart.

Abide

"Abide in Me, and I in You" John 15:4a

The word abide as it relates to abiding in Christ shows up five times in the fifteenth chapter of John, five times in 1 John and one time in 2 John. Jesus often used this sentence as He was teaching His disciples how to overcome their weaknesses and how to have victory over their circumstances. Significantly, He told His disciples to abide in Him several times as part of His last address before leaving this world.

As the Lord instructed His followers on how to become and remain fruitful, He told them to abide in Him.

The verb to abide in Hebrew, "meno" translates as "remaining in the same place over a period of time", or "wait for — remain in a place/state with expectancy concerning a future event", or yet "to continue, to remain in, to keep on."[1]

When the Lord told His disciples to abide in Him, He was indeed giving us the key to a victorious life in Him, regardless of our circumstances. There is no other way — if we try to overcome our weaknesses on our own strength and apart from Christ, we hopelessly fall into temptation.

Likewise, when we go through the darkest valleys in life, emotionally, physically or spiritually, it does not matter who is walking beside us, how much money we have or if the best doctor or therapist in town is on speed dial. If we are not plugged into the Source of all peace and wisdom, if we are not "remaining in Him" in obedience and trusting Him for deliverance, if we don't keep on keeping on by faith, we fail miserably.

Although "meno" sounds like a stationary state (to remain,) it is, in its core, an action verb, because it implies your willingness to stay and not move. You must CHOOSE to abide and not move. And I promise — you cannot remain fully plugged into the world and in Christ at the same time.

As I asked God to reveal the things in my life that were preventing me from having the abundant life that He has promised, I was honestly expecting the usual answer: read your Bible more, pray more. Instead, a strong conviction set in: I was feeding my mind with too much junk. Before anything else, I was to take inventory of what was allowed into my brain. Wholesome and faith-filled thoughts cannot thrive and win in a mind that is filled with garbage or empty thoughts.

Better yet, when life becomes challenging, TV celebrities will not help you overcome your circumstances. It won't matter how many followers you have on Twitter or how many likes your posts get. What will matter is how much truth you have in you. God's Word and songs of praise can bring you peace in the midst of life's storms.

So that is the first challenge I give you on this journey we are starting together:

What fills your mind every day? Do you find time not to miss one single episode of the latest reality show and yet, don't have time for God every day?

Can you miss reading your Bible at any day, but cannot imagine spending an afternoon without Facebook and Twitter?

What about music and movies? Have you grown accustomed to hearing people using profanity against God and His Son?

Do you browse websites that are not fit for a child of God?

These are questions that will indeed reveal the state of your heart and mind. And will answer this question:

Am I abiding in Christ and thriving…

Or is my mind starving?

Chapter 2

When Your Heart Believes Lies

*"The human heart is the most deceitful
of all things, and desperately wicked.
Who really knows how bad it is?"*
Jeremiah 17:9 (NLT)

Many of us believe lies that keep us from reaching our full potential. Lies about ourselves, engrained in our brains by what we were told as children; lies about how limited we are; lies which often overshadow our potential and consequently, our destiny. These lies often tell us that our circumstances will never change, or that our worth is in what we have or in what we accomplish, not in who we are as children of God.

We believe lies about God which were often taught by well-meaning people who were also misinformed about Him. These lies ultimately downplay His love, His grace and His power.

We believe lies about others. We believe some people to be so important that we emulate their bad choices. We let our immoral society often manipulate our thinking and allow its views to shape our self-image.

This chapter seeks to demystify the lies that we often believe.

And what better way to start, than to focus on the very creator of all lies. Satan is the one who makes war against God's children daily, often trying to persuade us into doubting God's goodness. He prowls as a hungry animal around us, looking for a small gap to invade our thoughts. And when he does, he masterfully cracks our Twelve-Inch Faith Bridge, as we start focusing on our feelings, rather than what we know about our God's omnipotence, love and grace.

We must learn to identify his strategies, if we are to build a strong faith bridge.

Satan's mighty weapon

Our mind is Satan's most effective weapon of war. As I often say, he's been around much longer than you and I and therefore he knows all human frailties. He discerns our weaknesses and what thoughts make us steer away from God's truth.

Everyone has an Achilles heel — that awesome weakness in spite of overall strength, which can potentially lead to our downfall.

To me, personally, it's my health.

I've had major health issues in the past eight years. In 2006, when our youngest daughter was only six months old, I had a major intestinal surgery. Following the surgery, I developed a myriad of gastric issues. For three years I was tested for different diseases, while doctors were clueless of what was wrong with me. I had no energy and any small effort would wipe me out.

Then in June, 2009, someone finally gave it a name. I had celiac disease, which is easily managed by a gluten-free diet. However, because I was unaware of the allergy and had eaten gluten all my life, the disease had taken a toll in my body. I started a grueling gluten-free diet, which is no cupcake (no pun intended!) and started feeling better after several weeks.

Everything was fine until June 2010, when I had another major surgery, a hysterectomy this time. Although these issues were aggravating and certainly took a toll on my body, I kept things in perspective. God had brought me through it all. At least it wasn't cancer! I navigated the rough waters, for the most part, with a smile on my face and a steadfast faith.

Then on February 8, 2012, I woke up with an annoying abdominal discomfort that turned into excruciating pain by midday. The pain was very similar to what I had felt when a diverticula burst in my intestines, sending me to the hospital for emergency surgery six years earlier. I called my doctor, who rushed me to the ER for an image of my abdomen.

As the doctor came back from reading the results of the CT scan, his face was somber. The pain was due to an erupted ovarian cyst, which is not a big deal, really. But in the process of scanning my abdomen, they found a mass in my left kidney. I was urged to see an urologist immediately.

Two days later, the world spun around as I sat across the urologist who broke the news to me: I had kidney cancer.

Two months after kidney surgery, my brother-in-law tragically passed away in a plane crash. His wife, our sister-in-law, was left to manage their business on her own. So for the following nine months, we lived between Atlanta and Chattanooga, while working full time, taking care of our girls and trying to bring comfort to our sister-in-law as we helped her manage the business.

It was a very emotional time. Donnie was like a brother to me, but the worst part was seeing my husband, his family and especially our children suffer, as we tried to cope with our tragic loss.

Meanwhile, my health issues did not stop. Rather, it seemed like my saga with health problems spurred Satan to torment me. He started attacking my mind daily — hourly even, with thoughts of defeat and death.

I started doubting God. And that was a new valley, one I had never experienced before.

You see, during my journey with cancer, I was so very aware of God's grace to me.

Kidney cancer is a silent killer. Most of the people who have it, don't find out until it's too late. I was very aware that God had lavished His grace upon me in the form of an erupted ovarian cyst. The days before surgery and months afterwards stirred a renewed sense of gratitude in my heart.

However, the stressful months that followed Donnie's death drove my body and mind over the edge. Enough was enough. My body, and worse than that, my spirit crashed. And Satan danced all over it.

He started whispering lies.

"You'll die." "You won't see your children graduate." "You have something terrible inside you."

"Does God even exist?"

That, my friend, was cancer for my soul. It was the darkest trial I have ever experienced, bar none. Physical and emotional weariness opened a gap for months of strong spiritual attack.

You may have experienced a similar situation, when your biggest weakness became Satan's playground. It may have been tempting thoughts. It may have been a trial, like mine. Regardless, the first thing we must bear in mind is that he constantly uses our mind against us. As we become too tired, too tempted, or too ill, he comes with vengeance against God's children.

It's war. And it's real.

The second part of this book will help you learn how to overcome Satan's lies through the power of God's Word and prayer.

But at the moment, I'd like to address three other common lies that we often believe; lies which cloud our thoughts and prevent us from keeping strong faith during our journey on earth.

Believing lies about God

"See to it that no one takes you captive by philosophy and empty deceit, according to human tradition, according to the elemental spirits of the world, and not according to Christ." Colossians 2:8

I sat quietly on the pew, listening to the teacher as she explained about the relevance and meaning of the sacred ordinances of the church. Confession and communion were the subjects that day, as I attended the course that prepared me to receive my first communion as a 13-year old Catholic girl. I was the oldest in the group; most of my peers ranged in age from 8 to 10 years old.

My parents believed it to be crucial that I understood the importance and decided to take the communion on my own, therefore they let me decide when to take the course.

Today I realize that my decision was more based on peer pressure than religious conviction. After all, I was the only seventh grader who would not take the communion wafers during the masses held at our Catholic school.

However, there was another reason that haunted me. I was afraid that God was angry because I chose not to partake in the Lord's Supper and that He would condemn me to purgatory, or hell, for not accepting His ordinance. Truth being told, I was taught to believe I was to be afraid of God. I am sure that was never the intention of the well-meaning people who taught me about Him in those early years, but that was the message I understood. Thus I grew up with many misconceptions and errors about the Father's character.

Fast forward thirty years and, although my understanding of His Word, salvation and the vastness and riches of His grace has certainly changed, and although today I fear Him, as in respect, instead of being afraid, I wonder how many times I am still tempted to believe lies about God.

Do you find that is evident in your life, too?

One of the biggest lies we are tempted to believe is that, when something bad happens to one of God's children, that must mean that the child is living out of His will.

This is often a lie from the devil.

Naturally, there are situations in which the trials we face are just a consequence of our disobedience or neglect. Smoking increases a chance of lung cancer. Adultery destroys families. You get the picture.

But then there are times when God allows the trials, not to harm us or destroy us, but to mold, strengthen and cleanse us. Often, too, trials are used by God to teach us humility.

"Then Jesus was led by the Spirit into the wilderness to be tempted by the devil." Matthew 4:1

Jesus' forty days in the wilderness were undoubtedly one of the most trying times of the Savior's journey on earth. He was hungry, thirsty and weak. And then, just to make things worse, Satan showed up to tempt Him. We all know the passage and rejoice in the Savior's victory over the devil. Nevertheless, this significant information, intentionally stated in the three gospels that narrate the account, hold a very important key to the temptation of Christ: "He was led by the Spirit to be tempted by the devil."

The wilderness experience was crucial for Jesus' preparation to fulfill God's perfect plan for His life. It was the onset of His ministry. It was His blessed preparation ground for what lay ahead for Him. He was led to the wilderness by the Father Himself, in order to be strengthened for the task ahead of Him. He was led to the wilderness to be tempted to quit and yet, not give up. Instead, He came out of it ready to start the ministry that would change the world forever.

Likewise, if you are a child of God, obedient to His Word, your wilderness is not accidental. God led you there. You did not necessarily fall there because you disobeyed. You might just need to be there.

The challenge is to take our focus out of our well being and look beyond, into eternity.

God is not a genie. His main purpose is not to make us happy. His main purpose is to make us become more like Christ. In the process, there will be pain. There will be trials and temptations.

God is inviting you to look into this special detail about your wilderness: He led you there. He has invited the trials and temptations that you may go through, as devastating as they may seem, to be used as tools to shape you into the person He wants you to become, thus empowering you to fulfill His plan for your life.

Don't believe the lie. God is still good when the worst happens. Though our circumstances may have tossed us about like the waves of a raging sea, God's love and goodness never change, because He never changes.

He is forever merciful. Forever good.

But He loves you too much to leave you as you are.

And that, my friend, is no lie.

Believing lies about yourself

It was almost ten o'clock at night. I was tired and a bit grouchy. When the commercial played, I rolled my eyes, annoyed. Another miraculous skin rejuvenating product, promising to restore my skin's radiance and make my crow's feet vanish in 8 weeks. The gorgeous model's face beamed on the screen. The problem was the kid's age. She had to be about twenty.

Wait 'til you hit forty, sweetie, I thought.

There's a reason why billions of dollars are spent yearly on the cosmetics industry. Many of us are plagued by thoughts of inadequacy, instilled in us when we were still very young. We believe lies about how we should look, or perform, and because of that, we spend our lives trying to measure up.

Whether it is about appearance, performance or intellectual ability, people believe lies about themselves every single day. When we choose to accept these lies as truth, a vicious cycle starts: Either we grow up with a very poor self-image, or we inadvertently live trying to hit an unrealistic mark, thus becoming perfectionists. On either end of the spectrum, we live to depend much on ourselves or external circumstances, thus allowing little room for God and faith.

Have you bought it hook, line and sinker?

The teacher's French accent didn't help. It was hard to understand her, keep up with her small tambourine beats and remember that the legs and arms had coordinating movements.

"Plié" "pas de bourrée ouvert," bang! Her tambourine would hit my bottom again. *"Posturrre, Patricia!"* "Tuck your bellyee!"

I would look at her favorite pupil in dismay. She was graceful, lean and so very flexible. The teacher's smile brightened when she stopped by her side. I was nine years old and I wanted to be a ballerina for my daddy. He was an artist and loved everything classic. In her day, Madame Nicolle had been the grand Rio de Janeiro ballet company's first ballerina. My dad has seen her perform several times while living in Rio as a young man.

She had moved to our small town and to be in her prestigious ballet classes was every little girl's dream. But my dream quickly shattered as I realized I did not have the talent, or the physique, to be a prima ballerina.

I was going through that common phase in a young girl's life when, although still a child, the body starts changing. I was not skinny at all. My dad had always connected a woman's beauty with a lean figure and I knew that. That was not me! And, although I am certain dad never meant any harm, I believed I was chubby. I believed the lie.

I started a self-deprecating cycle. I cannot remember ever not being on a diet. I tried them all!

Today I look at my pictures through the years and I see a healthy, slim girl — whose mirror told her she was fat.

My story is very common. Many men and women live in defeat because of lies they believe. Intentionally or unintentionally, we're exposed to skewed views about ourselves that we often embrace as truth. Because of that, many shy away from a victorious, vibrant life due to low self-esteem. Instead of embracing what God says about us, we take the bait, feeling inadequate, ugly, and useless.

If this is a familiar scenario, I am here to tell you that there is life beyond the lie. God wants to set you free from the bondage of defeat and embrace what He says about you.

He crafted you in your mother's womb. He redeemed you. He loves you unconditionally. Inadequacy does not fit a child of the King of Kings. It is a lie that you must confront, if you are to live Jesus' promised abundant life.

There is another side of the spectrum as a result of believing lies about ourselves. It can be as damaging and crippling as low self-esteem. As a matter of fact, it is often a cry of those who desperately need approval.

It is called perfectionism.

The perils of perfectionism

Perfectionism, in psychology, is a personality trait characterized by a person's striving for flawlessness and setting excessively high performance standards, accompanied by overly critical self-evaluations and concerns regarding others' evaluations. It is best conceptualized as a multidimensional characteristic, as psychologists agree that there are many positive and negative aspects. In its maladaptive form, perfectionism drives people to attempt to achieve an unattainable ideal, and their adaptive perfectionism can sometimes motivate them to reach their goals. In the end, they derive pleasure from doing so. When perfectionists do not reach their goals, they often fall into depression. (Wikipedia definition)

I am not a psychologist, but we know that the need to be "perfect" is very real to many people, and often especially to women. Also, if we become mothers, the bar is raised to new heights. It's as if on the day our first bundle of joy arrived, we received two special "genes" to be added to motherhood: guilt and comparison. And sometimes, sister perfectionism might tag along for the ride.

You may have had the burden to have been raised by parents who set high performance standards. Or it may be that you are so insecure and you drive yourself crazy trying to reach higher and higher standards. Regardless, perfectionism is a burden.

It's a monster, disguised in party clothes.

Perfectionism cries out: "I'm not good unless I'm perfect." That cry is often a result of a life permeated by self-deprecating lies about oneself, and unrealistic perception about others.

There are several faces of perfectionism:

Physical perfectionism, which plagues men and women who cannot accept aging (or their physical appearance, period).

Don't get me wrong. I echo my pastor Dr. Charles Stanley's motto: *Do your best, look your best, be your best.* I believe we are to take care of our bodies, the temple of the Holy Spirit, by eating healthy, exercising when we can and living a healthy life-style. But there is a point when the focus is so intense in how we look, that it becomes an idol. As we become obsessed with appearance, we often forget to nurture internal beauty. And as superficial as our attitude becomes, so does our faith. The more we focus on the external, the less time we give to the eternal.

Consequently, we find it hard to maintain our Twelve-Inch Faith Bridge intact because we forfeit spending time developing two crucial tools that we need to be victorious: Our relationship with the Father and knowledge of His Word.

Another form of perfectionism is:

Performance perfectionism, which plagues people by the concept that they have to be perfect in all they do. This trait is often found in people who were often compared to others: their siblings, the little girl next door, the high school athlete- you name it. When they are grown, their home needs to look a certain way, their spouses are never good enough and their children are never quite up to their standards. Their hair is always in place and they won't leave the house without makeup. They have a hard time accepting a B on their child's report card and they are always criticizing their friends.

Performance perfectionists have a hard time believing that God loves them unconditionally, therefore they either have a hard time admitting their sins and flaws, or live a defeated life, since essentially, no one is perfect but God.

Spiritual Perfectionism —The perfectionists of the Bibles are also known as the Pharisees. Perfectionism goes together with legalism, pride and judgmentalism.

"Woe to you, teachers of the law and Pharisees, you hypocrites! You give a tenth of your spices—mint, dill and cummin. But you have neglected the more important matters of the law — justice, mercy and faithfulness. You should have practiced the latter, without neglecting the former. You blind guides! You strain out a gnat but swallow a camel" (Matthew 23:23-24).

We often criticize religions and cults which promote that in order to be saved we must "perform". Truth be told, Christians also often make the mistake of overloading themselves with "good works", forfeiting true worship.

God is not impressed with my performance. He wants my heart. A heart that understand that my perfection is only found in Him. Our good works should be a natural response of a heart that loves others and wants to please the Father: "For it is by grace you have been saved, through faith—and this not from yourselves, it is the gift of God — not by works, so that no one can boast. For we are God's workmanship, created in Christ Jesus to do good works, which God prepared in advance for us to do" (Ephesians 2:8-10).

Nevertheless, what does the Bible say about perfectionism?

First of all, it is a hoax in itself. Perfectionism often involves raising the bar to absurd heights and striving in our own efforts for something that only God can do.

It is true that the Bible calls us to be "perfect as [our] heavenly Father is perfect" (Matthew 5:48).

However, the Greek word for "perfect" here is *telios*. It means *"brought to its end, completed, or perfect."* So, to be "perfect" in this sense is not how perfectionists so often imagine it. Rather, it is to be completed in Christ. Philippians 1:6 says that completion is the work of God. He created us, saved us, and is faithful to perfect us. "And I am certain that God, who began the good work within you, will continue his work until it is finally finished on the day when Christ Jesus returns."

Perfectionism may appear to be wise, but its wisdom has no spiritual value: (Colossians 2:20-23). "Since you died with Christ to the basic principles of this world, why, as though you still belonged to it, do you submit to its rules: 'Do not handle! Do not taste! Do not touch!'? These are all destined to perish with use, because they are based on human commands and teachings. Such regulations indeed have an appearance of wisdom, with their self-imposed worship, their false humility and their harsh treatment of the body, but they lack any value in restraining sensual indulgence."

Meaning that our attempt to be perfect will never change the condition of our hearts. The lie is, we can measure up on our own. The truth is — without God's guidance and grace, all our efforts to reach perfection are useless.

The point of the gospel is that we are unable to be perfect. We all "fall short"; we all "miss the mark" (Romans 3:23). Sinners need a Savior, and that's why Jesus came. When we trust in Him, He forgives our shortcomings, imperfections, and iniquities. We can stop striving for an arbitrary, worldly "perfection" and rest in the Perfect One (Matthew 11:28).

Believing lies about others

"She is so gorgeous, Mom!"

My daughter stood in front of the cashier's checkout line, surveying all the magazines. She pointed out to one of the beautiful Hollywood's actresses whose life has been shattered by drug abuse, compulsive dieting and a revolving door of boyfriends.

"Yes, she is beautiful, honey. And miserable."

And yet, so many young girls want to be just like her, I thought.

We believe lies about others. Proof of that is the growing number of reality shows that entertain America nowadays. I find it quite amusing that they are called reality. There is little reality about them. Most are designed to sell a lie. Whether from reality shows, or the airbrushed pictures on magazines, many believe that some celebrities have what it takes to make them happy. They take the bait and believe the lie, spending their days trying to look like or obtain it.

The truth is that the grass is not always greener on the other side. It's the same grass, with a fence separating you from them. Often that fence that separates us are choices, such as what morals or ethics we are willing to give up in order to obtain what others have, or what sacrifices a family must make to finance the latest or the greatest.

Our fence should separate us, indeed. But the standards we should raise with it should be given by God, not others. We should never allow others to dictate how we feel about ourselves. And yet, many of us do. We believe that they are better than we are and because we believe that lie, we follow standards and choices that were never designed to be ours.

Worse yet, we make their same wrong choices.

We live in an age of moral relativeness, where everything is permissible, so long as it does not hurt others. Our society's moral compass has shifted immensely in the past fifty years. We are told that, unless we accept immoral choices as truth, we become intolerant, ignorant, even hateful.

That is another lie.

We must love people, not their sin. Jesus walked among the worst of His day: adulterers, tax collectors, blasphemers, to name a few. He loved them, but He always confronted their sinful condition with truth. We should do the same.

To be like Jesus is to reject the lie that sin is ok, extend loving arms to those who believed the lie and tell them this truth:

God loves you too much to leave you as you are.

The consequences of believing the lies

"I'll be first in line to talk to Eve when I get to heaven."

That's a joke that I always tell my friends when referring to the hard times women go through with choices, hormones, and children. We are often hard on Eve because she gave in to Satan's lies.

And yet, we have all fallen into the same trap:

"Did God really say?"

"Does God really love me?"

"Is that really sin?"

Lies can be devastating to our spiritual lives, no matter which lies we choose to believe. We cannot truly love, or trust a tyrant God. Do we believe that He is all good, all merciful and all powerful? If so, we must confront the lies with truth. The Bible has a truth antidote for every lie that we believe. We must choose to take God at His Word and tell our hearts the truth about our God, as well as about ourselves.

"In reference to your former manner of life, you lay aside the old self, which is being corrupted in accordance with the lusts of deceit, and that you be renewed in the spirit of your mind, and put on the new self, which in the likeness of God has been created in righteousness and holiness of the truth. Ephesians 4:22-24

If we are to live an abundant, victorious life, regardless of our circumstances, we must take every defeating or immoral thought captive into the knowledge of who we are in Christ (2 Corinthians 10:5): Redeemed. Loved. Equipped for each battle.

Victorious!

That is the life-giving truth of the Gospel.

Chapter 3

Pet Hurts: When you are Enslaved to your Past

"Do not call to mind the former things, or ponder things of the past.
"Behold, I will do something new, now it will spring forth;
will you not be aware of it?" Isaiah 43:18

Doctors' offices are filled with patients suffering from depression, anxiety and numerous other psychological disorders. The pharmaceutical industry thrives in selling medications that promise to help men, women and even children deal with emotional, physical and psychological stress. If we were to evaluate most of these patients, I believe we would quickly conclude that many of them have past traumas and unresolved emotional wounds that prevent them from thriving in life.

According to the American Psychological Association,(APA,) the consequences of repressed anger, bitterness and instability drive millions of Americans to the drug stores each year. A stunning $11 billion dollars of revenue was received by the pharmaceutical giants for antidepressants alone in 2010.[1]

Many of such cases are people who live chained to their past. They can't seem to let it go. And unfortunately, many of us can relate to their story.

There are many Christians who cannot thrive in their faith walk because they don't seem to be able to let go of their past. We may live in bondage to past sins, hurts and traumas, so much so that they become like a pet to us: we feed them, pamper them and often refuse to do something to overcome them and let them go.

However, if we are to build a strong Twelve-Inch Faith Bridge, rising above our past is an absolute must.

In this chapter, I would like to discuss issues regarding damaging feelings that develop into strongholds and keep us bound to our past and ineffective for God: unforgiveness, broken relationships and negative past experiences. Indeed, these heavy concerns have the ability to crack the foundation of our very Twelve-Inch Faith Bridge.

If we believe that "God works all things together for good for those who love Him and are called according to His purpose" (Romans 8:28), then we must believe that God wants us to gather wisdom from our past experiences, forgive those who wronged us and use our testimony to strengthen our faith and point others to Him for deliverance.

But how do we do it? How can we be set free from our past, forgive ourselves and those who wronged us and let our pet hurts go?

I'd like to first illustrate how we allow our past traumas and experiences to shape how we respond to the present. Healing can only start when we identify that we have a problem. Recognizing and acknowledging the issue is the beginning of healing.

Dragging a heavy load

Our conversation was going well. We talked about the girls' school, the weather and then our concerns about the country and the economy.

I had learned to keep our conversations quite superficial. But unfortunately, we had enough time in our hands for the inevitable. The past was knocking at the door and my friend just had to let it in.

Have you ever been around someone who just cannot let go of the past? Has it ever been you?

These types of personalities can be met everywhere and each family has at least one. They drag their shackles around everywhere they go. They are slaves and do not know it. They are unhappy and invariably become bitter, resentful … and lonely. So.very.lonely.

They are doctors and housewives, wealthy and poor. Many of them sit on the pew right beside us. Many even know Jesus as their Savior. And yet, for different reasons, they choose to remain chained to the misery of their past, even though they know that Jesus came to set them free.

My heart aches for them.

But truthfully, as I mentioned before, many of us have been there. I know I have.

For years I looked back to find justification for my bad attitude and shallow faith. I would blame my insecurities on my parent's broken marriage and my poor self-image on things that I heard growing up. I blamed my jealousy on that boyfriend who was unfaithful and my reluctance in giving up bad habits on the fact that I was raised in a more liberal culture.

Blame, blame, blame.

Attached to the chains that keep us bound to our past is the Blame Monster. And we feed it every time we drag the past around, allowing it to rob us of an abundant, successful present and future.

Honestly, it's not easy to release the past. And I cannot in all fairness compare my own, however painful, experiences with some other terrible stories which I've heard. But regardless of the measure of our pain, eventually we must be confronted with two simple questions:

"Am I willing to let go?"

and

"Is God able to rewrite ANY story?"

33

Sometimes it is easier to bring the past along with us, because in order to confront it, we must realize our share of responsibility over our destiny. Of course, there are things that happen that are absolutely outside of our control: A child never does anything to justify abuse nor the onset of severe illness. Neither is it one's fault that a parent dies nor leaves home, abandoning his or her family. These are truly traumatic experiences, brought on people every day by decisions of which they had no control.

However, there are hurts of the past that have a measure of self-infliction which is hard to confront. It's easier to continue blaming mom and dad, or the ex-husband or ex-wife, than looking within ourselves, asking God to help us and allowing Him to teach us how to move forward and take ownership of our destiny.

There is also the fact that we become accustomed to living in bondage. We may have blamed the circumstances in our past for so long, that we do not know how to survive without the dysfunction! Ouch. What a painful truth to some of us!

Of course! If you've been used to blame someone for your current misery, even if what they did to you is long in the past, it becomes very hard to let it go, or choose to change the subject and turn the page.

Set them free!

I was resting in bed upstairs as I recovered from a major surgery. My children's laughter reached the bedroom and woke me up. They were giggling of excitement as grandma once again came up with a new, creative way to play with them.

I smiled and uttered a prayer of thanksgiving for my mom. Once again, this loving woman had dropped everything in her life and had flown 6,000 miles to take care of me and my family in a time of need. Regardless of distance, time or cost, I know that as long as God gives her breath, I can always count on my mom.

My mind goes back in time and I remember our relationship as I grew up. As many women of her day, mom had to work five days a week and sometimes on the weekends to help the family budget; therefore she was not very involved in our day-to-day activities. During the teenage years, as my parents' relationship became stormy, we were all victims in the consequences of a broken marriage. Hormones and anger made my young mind shut down to any common sense. The hurt of seeing my parents growing apart blinded any attempt to understand my mother and so our relationship became distant and shaky.

As we both struggled with our individual crisis, we hurt each other deeply. As in many other mother-daughter situations that I have known, there was pain, misunderstanding and incompatibility for far too many years.

Today, however, in spite of anything in the past, I can honestly say that Mom is a best friend. I long to see her and spend time with her. I love to hear her voice when I dial her number. And even though our personalities are pretty different and we don't always agree, our love and longing to be together grows deeper with each passing year.

Our secret?

We set each other free.

We can't help but grow old, but we have to choose to grow wiser

As a grown woman, I started to understand her longings, sorrows and disappointments. I often made myself put on her shoes to imagine her experiences.

When I became a Christian at 25, I realized for the first time that no one is worthy of forgiveness; however that is exactly what Christ offers to anyone who will ask. I also came to realize that true love never withholds forgiveness and that we cannot expect to be forgiven if we don't forgive others. This former Catholic school girl knew all too well the words of the Lord's Prayer in Luke 11: "And forgive us our sins, *as we forgive those who sin against us.*"

I know several mothers and daughters who are wasting time and missing out an abundant life with each other because of unforgiveness. I know daughters who dread the thought of being around their mother and mothers whose daughter can never measure up to their expectations. I know mothers who compete with their daughters and daughters who will never agree with their moms, even when they are absolutely right. The same occurs in different relationships where trust and dreams are shattered. Without forgiveness there is no factual restoration. Without restoration, our future is bound to defeat. Heaven shuts down. Our Faith Bridge stays broken and therefore nonfunctional.

As we stand in a position of self-righteousness, holding on to thirty year old grudges, we fail to realize that we are the ones held in bondage. Even if the person who wronged you has a hardened heart and continually hurts you, do yourself a favor: *Set them free!* Ask God to help you forgive them and pray for them. Extend the same forgiveness that you so long to receive from those you hurt.

I cannot remember exactly when it started, but somewhere along life's way, I started to choose to love my mom for whom she is. I don't try to change her and I don't look back anymore. I look forward to the years we have ahead of us. No matter how many we have, I am choosing, one step at a time, to fully, abundantly enjoy each one.

Regardless of who hurt you, whether it was a parent, spouse or friend, forgiving is not easy. Actually, I believe it's quite impossible without God. But with His help, you can.

Have you tried asking Him to help you overcome?

"With man this is impossible, but with God all things are possible."
Matthew 19:26

We are not our sins!

I've met several people along the years who claimed that they couldn't stop thinking about their past sins, those decisions they made before accepting Christ as their Savior. One particular friend suffered with self-depreciating thoughts for many years following her salvation. Although she believed God had cast her sins as far as the east is from the west (Psalm 103:12), she could not stop thinking about them and, consequently, felt undeserving of God's love.

Many people can relate to this experience. I believe it's more common among folks like me, who became Christians as adults. We (usually) come to Christ with many more regrets than someone who was saved at an early age.

Regardless of how old you were when you became a Christian, the concept of "self-forgiveness" is a dangerous one. It's dangerous because of its consequences to our spiritual lives. If we are to live victorious in Christ, we must confront the reasons as to why we cannot seem to release our past mistakes and take ownership of our New Creature nature, purchased with Jesus' precious blood at the cross.

Holding on to our past mistakes grieves God's heart. When we refuse to let go, we take a position that belong to God alone: we become judges.

In a very twisted way, we assume a position of self-righteousness.

You mean, God forgave you, but you can't forgive yourself? Really?

Indeed, saying that what you've done is beyond forgiveness is the same as telling Jesus that His blood was not enough. It's like believing that the blood of the perfect Lamb was not sufficient to spare you from the angel of death (Exodus 12:23). It's saying that you must add your own blood to the door posts. Just a little presumptuous, isn't it?

Constantly remembering the sins that you've committed may also mean that you aren't completely healed, or that you have not entirely overcome the temptations that haunted you in the past.

Constantly thinking that you're not worthy of love screams that God made a mistake when He chose you to become part of His family, because He IS love. (1 John 4:8)

In His best-selling book *The Christian Atheist,* author Craig Groeschel calls us to break the shackles of shame:

"Like Peter, (we) can break free from the cycle of shame. We live lives of private defeat, but God wants to renew our hearts and minds and to send us into His world as lights shining in the darkness. Like Peter, we can become convinced of the truth: namely, that we are not our sins. And we are also not what others have done to us.

Rather, we are what God says we are: His children. We are forgivable. We are Changeable. We are capable. We are moldable. And we are bound by the limitless love of God."[2]

One table, two men, renewed life and eternal damnation

It was time for the Passover celebration. Jerusalem was buzzing with Jews from everywhere, ready to receive forgiveness and restoration. The upper room was quiet with Jesus' words echoing in the hearts of His close friends.

He said His time had come.

Peter's heart was filled with grief. Judas' heart was full of greed. The Savior gave Peter the terrifying news that he would deny him three times that very night. He then told His disciples that one of them would betray Him. Judas knew all along that he would become the guilty one. As Judas kissed Yeshua's face, he knew he was sealing Jesus' fate. His sin was deliberate and carefully planned.

Peter, on the other hand, could not conceive in his heart that he would deny his best friend, his redeemer. Not long before, he had proclaimed Yeshua's deity to all who could hear it (Matthew 16:13-17). He loved Jesus and believed Him. He longed to follow Him. Only a few hours later, he risked his own life to save Him at Gethsemane (John 18:10). He had no real intention to betray the long awaited Messiah.

And yet, as the rooster crowed at dawn, guilt filled his heart. Three times had he denied His Lord. All in one fateful night.

As continue reading the Gospel, we see how each man's destiny was shaped by the response to his sin.

Although he had access to the same forgiveness and grace that you and I would have, Judas' guilt did not allow him to receive eternal life.

Peter, on the other hand, used his sin and Yahweh's forgiveness to move on and further the kingdom. He did not deny his wrong doing, but instead of using it to deepen the roots of self-deprecation and defeat, he used his experience to tell others of God's redeeming grace. I imagine Peter's overwhelming joy while writing his epistle, remembering the Master's forgiveness:

*"He personally carried our sins in his body on the cross
so that we can be dead to sin and live for what is right.
By his wounds you are healed." 1 Peter 2:24.*

That's the life-giving message of the cross. Not only did Jesus give His life to reconcile us with the Father. He carried our sins in His body also so that we can use our past to testify of His amazing grace, not to condemn us. By His priceless wounds we are HEALED. Forgiven. Period.

So, what is it going to be?

Will you keep carrying the weight of the past, allowing the devil to point his nasty finger at you, saying: "How dare YOU think you are worth anything?" and consequently, like Judas, choose (spiritual) death?

Or … will you contemplate His stretched arms on the cross and choose to accept the vastness of His love and all-encompassing grace?

He has already forgiven you and He has sent each one of your sins into the dark sea of amnesia. Now, for your own sake, will you leave them there?

"He will again have compassion on us; he will tread our iniquities underfoot. You will cast all our sins into the depths of the sea."
Micah 7:19 (NASB)

Remember: Satan is behind our tendency not to let go. We must understand that. Self-condemnation does not come from the cross. It comes from the one who did everything to prevent the cross.

We can choose to stay bound to our past and live defeated, or we can choose to use our experiences to strengthen us and build our testimony of deliverance. Then we can be used to give hope to people in bondage.

Undeniably, God can use our testimony of deliverance from a particular sin to strengthen others. That's one of the reasons you'll find former alcoholics helping alcoholics, former addicts helping addicts. There is nothing more powerful than the song of a redeemed life as it is being rebuilt.

Leave the past where it belongs.

What about people who magnify their past as the best time of their lives? Have you been around Christians who go on and on boasting about their fun times, the parties and worldly things that they were involved in before they became a Christian or before they started committing their lives more to Christ? These people remind me of the Jews in the Wilderness of Paran. The story is told on the eleventh chapter of the book of Numbers.

In this passage, the people of Israel started to complain to Moses about the type of food that God had provided for them. *"Manna! Nothing but manna!",* they cried.

One of the things that called my attention as I studied the background in this passage was their location. If the people were camped at the foot of Mount Horeb, they would have had some provision within their reach, such as herbs and vegetables. But in the wilderness of Paran, where they were located, they had no resources from which to draw. It was a desolate place. Therefore, their daily complaint should have quickly turned into worship with thanksgiving for it was obvious that the *manna* sent from heaven was nothing short of another miracle from almighty God.

Instead, with their eyes blinded by lust, they magnified the plentiful food in Egypt, as if God had made a horrendous mistake delivering them from slavery.

While in Egypt, they had complained about the burdens they were submitted to day and night, and when they find themselves eating *manna* in the wilderness, they start talking about Egypt as if they had lived there as royalty. They talked as if the food they ate while under Pharaoh's watch was theirs for free, evidently forgetting that they paid for it with their own freedom.

They remembered cucumbers, melons, leeks, onions and garlic as if they were precious, dainty foods, all along forgetting the slave masters' whip, the death and sorrow that surrounded their lives. How foolish!

*"We remember the fish which we used to eat free in Egypt,
the cucumbers and the melons and the leeks and the onions
and the garlic, but now our appetite is gone. There is nothing at all
to look at except this manna." (v.5 — NLT)*

Cucumbers, melons, leeks, onions and garlic? Oh, my!

If we are not careful, we may fall into the same mistake as the Jews did time and again. As we wander in our own wilderness at times, waiting for God's promises to be fulfilled in our lives, we may fall into Satan's trap of so focusing on our seemingly better past that we totally miss God's miracles of provision and deliverance in the present.

In verse 6, the Jews were complaining about the *manna* that they so admired when they first saw it. It was good food, indeed, it was heavenly food. It was free and enough was provided for what each family needed each day. Moreover, the *manna* came from the bounty of God. It was new every morning, just like God's mercies to us are (Lam 3:23). And yet, they despised God's provision.

Be careful to keep your past where it belongs. If you do not, you will magnify things that looked good, but at the end, might have cost you your freedom, your peace and your joy. Worse yet, you may miss the miracles of provision that God is sending your way now - provision for your body needs and for your soul longings, as you walk closely to Him in the desert.

Did someone hurt you? For your own sake, set him or her free! There is healing available to you, if only you open the chains of blame and guilt and extend to others the same grace and forgiveness that Jesus gave you at the foot of the cross.

Did you mess up and miss God's best for you? He has a new "best" for you, if you are willing to ask Him to forgive you and to show you the way. He is a God of second, third ... yes, unlimited chances!

Do you miss the "plenty" that you seemed to have before you started walking with God? Remember that all material things, human accomplishments and all the pleasures of this world are nothing compared to the promises and the glorious inheritance that we receive as we walk in obedience to our Maker.

Open your hands and let go. Stretch your arms upwards and let God fill your heart with His best. Let Him fill your cup with new things until it really overflows!

Indeed, the Bible's message of restoration rings the same from Genesis to Revelation: *"I am able to rewrite your story — any story. And I can make all things new, if only you are willing to let go."*

Just as He did to the woman at the well, who did not look back at years of promiscuity ... but rather, went on sharing her story of redemption in the city (John 4:7-27), He can do it for you.

Just as He did to Joseph, who did not cling to the years of slavery and imprisonment, but looked forward to the fulfillment of God's promises given to him in a dream (Genesis 37:5-9), Jesus can do it for you.

And also, just as He did to the woman with the alabaster box, who poured her past and her pain at the Savior's feet ... the One who could give her the hope of a new future (Luke 7:37-38), He will cleanse your past to make you ready for a bright tomorrow.

"I came that you may have life and have it abundantly", He says.

He does not offer to erase the past, but to heal and restore us completely, if only we are willing to cut the chains and let the past go.

That is the part of our story that is absolutely, unquestionably, in our hands.

No one can do it for us. We must choose to leave the past where it belongs, so that we may receive God's abundant future.

Chapter 4

When you hang out with the wrong crowd

"No man is an island, entire of itself; every man is a piece of the continent, a part of the main." John Donne (Meditation VXII)

John Donne was a famous English poet and cleric (priest) of the Church of England in the seventeenth century. He wrote the famous quote "No man is an island" while battling a disease that eventually claimed his life. He wrote the acclaimed "Meditations" as he pondered life, sickness, health and relationships at what he correctly projected was near the end of his journey on earth. The quote has since been used in poetry, music and art in general, to reinforce the fact that we cannot do life alone.[1]

This is a mighty truth — family and friends greatly influence how we respond to life. Give a child a good, healthy environment and that child will thrive. Surround a child with bad influence and that child will have little chance to succeed and make wise decisions.

I have a personal testimony of this truth.

Raised by middle class Brazilian parents, my upbringing was marked by love and sacrifice on my parents' part. Mom and Dad worked hard to be able to provide a good education for their children. In Brazil, the pinnacle of good education was attending Catholic schools. And so I was raised attending masses at school and knowing the ordinances of the church. My parents were nonpracticing Catholics, which simply meant that they professed the Catholic faith but did not attend mass.

By the time I turned thirteen, my parents' marriage had deteriorated to an unsustainable relationship. The environment at home wasn't the best. It was a confusing, difficult time for all of us. To make matters worse, my hormones were flaring at the dawn of adolescence.

That's when I fled to busyness.

Drama club, volleyball, piano lessons, English lessons, Cub Scouts leader — As I look back, the list of activities is pretty overwhelming. But these activities provided purpose and objectiveness to my confused heart. I didn't see it then, but today it is clear to me that God, in His mercy, was protecting me by keeping me busy.

"An empty mind is the devil's workshop", my mom would say.

As usual, time proved Mom to be right.

But as I look back and contemplate those days, I can also remember some of my friends who had lives that were as busy, parents who also had little time for their children, and yet, those kids made terrible decisions that impacted their lives for years to come: drugs, teenage pregnancy, car accidents due to drunk driving. These were kids who attended the same school, the same programs. They sat on the same pews as the nuns taught us discipline and the fear of the Lord. And yet, they chose to say "yes" to the wrong choices.

What happened?

I was supposed to be the kid who took the wrong turn, right?

My parents were divorcing.

My sister had left home.

I was confused and I needed escape. I needed approval. I needed love. And, to help me handle these emotions, it wouldn't be hard to reach for something that would help me feel numb.

These are all perfect ingredients for teenage bad decisions. And still, I did not make them. No drugs. No teenage sex. I kept good grades and a good reputation in spite of what I experienced at the time.

Why were my decisions not life-shattering?

First I have to give my parents credit. Although their marriage failed, they never failed their kids. I never felt as if I wasn't loved. And although they didn't become Christians until later in life, they also taught me good morals and ethics, both in words and action, even during their hardest trials.

But then there is an influence that I firmly believe became key: I had good, moral friends.

"Do not be misled. 'Bad company corrupts good character'"
1 Corinthians 15:33

"Diga-me com quem andas que direi quem és"
"Tell me who you hang out with and I'll tell you who you are." I'd be a rich woman if I had a dollar for each time I heard this from my mom as a teenager.

Mom was right again. As much as a good friend can help a person make wise decisions, foolish or negative companions can bring us down and steer away us away from walking wisely with God.

In the midst of the storms that assailed my life, I had good friends. The kids I hung out with wanted to do what was right. They were not rebellious. We had fun, as teenagers do. But it was clean fun. I stayed away from the wrong crowd. And I believe my environment determined much of the outcome of those tumultuous years.

At that time in my life, the "wrong crowd" was easy to spot. But it's not always that easy.

Indeed, we often think of the *wrong crowd* only as the drug addicts or immoral, but that is not always the case. Unfortunately, their bad influence is not always so blunt.

As a matter of fact, when it comes to helping us keep our faith strong, the "wrong crowd" can be members of our families and childhood friends. They may sit on the pew next to us and attend the same Bible studies. They are often people we have known for a long time and therefore it is hard to separate ourselves from them. However, because of their attitude and choices in life, they can be a huge part of the reason why we find it hard to received God's best in life.

There are many traits in a friend that should warn us of their bad influence. My purpose in the chapter is to help you identify those traits in the people around you, and help you realize how much they impact the way you respond to your circumstances and how much their weight contributes to cracking your faith bridge.

The pessimist next door

"He spoke in the presence of his brothers and the wealthy men of Samaria and said, "What are these feeble Jews doing? Are they going to restore (the wall) for themselves? Can they offer sacrifices? Can they finish in a day? Can they revive the stones from the dusty rubble even the burned ones?" Now Tobiah the Ammonite was near him and he said, "Even what they are building — if a fox should jump on it, he would break their stone wall down!" Nehemiah 4:2-3

Of all bad companions, naysayers are probably among the ones who can do the greatest harm.

Nehemiah had been charged with the task of rebuilding the walls of Jerusalem. He knew the task wouldn't be easy. He was appointed by God for the challenge and started gathering the right people, placing them in strategic positions to rebuild the wall which would guard the unprotected city of Jerusalem.

As you read the first and second chapters of Nehemiah, the challenging task of rebuilding the wall takes form as each person is dedicated to a portion of the wall in a beautiful lesson of organized engineering design.

Everything is running like a clock. Yet, when we turn to chapter 4, we find Sanballat and Tobiah, the Ammonite, angrily trying to discourage Nehemiah and his workmen from finishing their God-given task. The text does not say it, but it seems as if Nehemiah knew these men pretty well. They tried everything they could to get him and his workers distracted:

"The wall is weak!" "You are weak!" "It will take too long!" "Who do you think you are?"

They carried on and on, arguing against the Jews' desire to carry out God's plan.

I can look back in my life and recount situation after situation when people tried to discourage me to do what needed to be done, or to fulfill God's direction for my life.

Had I listened to the naysayers along the way, I would not have married my husband … nor would I have moved across the continent to a foreign country. Had I listened to them, I would have stopped my ministry after writing the very first devotional. Had I listened to the naysayers, I would not have said yes to God on so many things that did not make sense, but which I knew were His will for my life.

Likewise, had Nehemiah and his workmen listened to the naysayers, they would have believed their lies, stopped the work and not carried out God's task.

Can you identify them in your life? The naysayers sneer at your God-given visions. They say that what you're doing is wrong. They'll spot the bad in every good.

Ultimately, given the right circumstances, they have the potential to sap your energy and your willingness to press on.

At the sight of the pessimist next door, you have three options: Believe them, leave them, or disregard them. Whether you can leave them or not, depends on the type of relationship and is something only you can decide.

Remember I am talking about friends, not your spouse or a relative. Some of these relationships cannot be ended. But with God's help, you can choose to disregard their negativity. There is no dishonor in that.

Therefore, if God gave you a charge and even if it looks impossible and some people in your life are saying you are nuts for doing it — do as Nehemiah and his workers did — Keep on working until you finish the task. And if your well-meaning "friends" call you to come down from your wall and feast with them, remember Nehemiah's words to Sanballat and Tobiah as he replied to their invitation to party:

"I am doing a great work and I cannot come down. Why should the work stop while I leave it and come down to you?" Nehemiah 6:3

If you are doing what God has told you to do, whatever you do — DO NOT COME DOWN!

Let the naysayers carry on. Even if your hard labor seems to bear little fruit, DO NOT COME DOWN!

You'll know you've overcome the pessimist's influence when you keep carrying on wherever God leads you, following His directions, step by step.

You are doing a great work. Whatever you do, don't listen to your Sanballats and Tobiahs. Just carry on building that wall!

The gossip

> *"Whoever goes about slandering reveals secrets, but he who is trustworthy in spirit keeps a thing covered." Proverbs 11:13*

Backbiter, busybody, slanderer, talebearer, whisperer — these are some of the terms used in the Bible to describe gossipers. None of them are flattering.

None of them evoke the thought of an ideal friend.

Even as you read these words, someone came to your mind. To some of you, if you are honest, that someone may be yourself. We've all been around friends who love to talk about others in a negative way. We all know people who cannot seem to keep a secret to save their lives.

And yet, we often turn a blind eye to their infidelity, and keep sharing our deepest longings with them.

Is your friend able to keep secrets? Does she itch to criticize someone? I believe this is a major issue with many women. Honestly, think about it: if Mary tells you Sarah's secret ... or if she speaks ill of Sarah behind her back, would it be possible that she does the same about you when you are not around? Exactly!

True friends give each other the courtesy of keeping secrets and not sharing private information. Period.

Gossipers are usually envious people. By bringing others down, they hope to diminish their own inadequacies and therefore feel better about themselves.

Now I must ask — who wants to call envy a friend? Envy cannot be a true friend, because it usually hates who you are and what you have.

Conversely, true friendship rejoices with your accomplishments instead of diminishing them. A true friend rejoices when you're successful, when you find true love, start a ministry or get promoted. A true friend rejoices when you're in spotlight, even if she or he is not.

Indeed, the state of our hearts when we see others conquering milestones that we wish for ourselves reveal much on the depth of our love for our neighbor.

We must identify the gossips in our lives, as hurtful as it may be. We then must decide whether we will allow their negative influence to shape our view of others and our effectiveness as Christians. We must either confront them or distance ourselves from them.

The only thing that is not an option is to mingle with them and become one of them.

God cannot bless an envious and unfaithful heart.

The immoral

I'd like to take us back to the book of Numbers, Chapter 11. In the previous chapter, we discussed how the Jews' covetousness blinded them and made them magnify the food in Egypt, all along forgetting about the years of painful slavery under Pharaoh's ironclad rule.

What I'd like to show you is that there was a mighty influence underlying God's people disposition in the wilderness:

"The rabble with them began to crave other food, and again the Israelites started wailing and said, "If only we had meat to eat! We remember the fish we ate in Egypt at no cost — also the cucumbers, melons, leeks, onions and garlic. But now we have lost our appetite; we never see anything but this manna!" Numbers 11:4

The whining goes on and on. It is indeed not a pretty picture, mainly because unfortunately, most of us can relate to it at some point in our history. The people of Israel were basing their heart's attitude on skewed views, which neglected God's goodness and past performance. As we look closely into this passage, we can learn important lessons from Israel's ingratitude towards God and the way they responded to their circumstances, even though they had seen God deliver and provide for them time and again.

On the particular verse above, there's an important detail not to be missed. Notice that the people who started the complaints were part of the "foreign rabble" that was traveling with the Israelites. These people were not God's people. They hitch-hiked along with God's people, so to speak, as He freed them from Egyptian bondage. These people were along for the ride towards the land of promise, but they were not willing to go through the state of probation necessary to get there.

They were like the sick sheep that infected the flock.

They were like the medieval plagues, which started in the outskirts of the cities where filthiness and poverty reigned, and quickly took over the palaces, killing the mighty and wealthy.

Indeed, this foreign rabble walked along God's people but not with God's people, and therefore their lust quickly spread and infected Israel's attitude. As they moaned and complained about what they did not have, their faithless viewpoint clouded God's children's perception of reality.

Hence, all of a sudden, Egypt turned into paradise!

Unfortunately, this type of "infection" isn't uncommon amongst God's people today. There are many Christians who are being infected by the ungodly. I know that I am perceived as a radical by some, but I cannot help but believe as I read the Bible, that the only way to be light in the world is if you keep your light shining brightly. It must be noted constantly that while we must live in the world, we don't have to live as the world. If we react and behave as the general world, our light cannot help but be dimmed to dullness.

That is a mighty and common danger — to be infected by the world rather than affecting our world for Christ. As we are immersed in the worldly and fleshly influence that permeates society, we end up measuring ourselves up to their standards, instead of emulating God's ways. Before we know it, we talk like them, dress like them and invariably, we act like them.

"You are the light of the world. A city set on a hill cannot be hidden. Nor does anyone light a lamp and put it under a basket, but on the lamp stand, and it gives light to all who are in the house. Let your light shine before men in such a way that they may see your good works, and glorify your Father who is in heaven."
Matthew 5:14-16 (NLT)

The only way we can be light is if we shine from within.

So if we are unable to stand among the unbelievers without being contaminated by their ways, their viewpoints and behaviors, we must choose to stay away until we are so immersed by God's light that their choices will not affect us. Rather, as they look at our lives, they'll be attracted and interested in knowing more about our Savior.

Only then, can you call yourself light.

Dare to choose to invest in true friendships. And if needed, yes, choose to distance yourself from those whose attitudes only make it harder for your Faith Bridge to stay strong.

On another chapter of *The Christian Atheist*, Craig Groeschel illustrates the importance of becoming aware of our friends' bad influence ... and doing something about it:

"As you overcome (...), you'll also want to cut any ties that might hold you down. (...) If you are surrounded by naysayers or others dangerous to your progress, ditch them. Surround yourself with new, good friends.

For example, if you're overcoming your problem with lust, and your buddies are going to strip clubs or have pornographic magazines lying around in their apartments, you need new friends. If you're determined to drop thirty pounds, but your friend Alicia keeps showing up with two pints of Ben and Jerry's Triple Caramel Chunk ice cream, Alicia needs to go. If you're striving to please God with your life, but the person you're dating continues to push you to do things you know you shouldn't, it's time to throw that little fish back in the pond."[2]

For someone out there, it may just be time to throw an entire school of fish back in the pond.

When two are better than one

"Two are better than one, because they have a good return for their work: If one falls down, his friend can help him up. But pity the man who falls and has no one to help him up! Also, if two lie down together, they will keep warm. But how can one keep warm alone?"
Ecclesiastes 4:9-11

I looked up and they were all standing together in that tiny room. Six people that I have learned to love as dear friends. Their eyes were full of concern and compassion. Their words were healing balm to my tired spirit. As they started praying, hands on my shoulder, I let tears of gratitude fall. "Thank you, God, for my friends," I whispered.

What would I do without friends?

I have thought about that often these days. When I moved to America, thirty years of my life were packed in four not-so-large suitcases. Mixed emotions flowed freely as we landed on Hartsfield-Jackson on

November 27th, 1999. There was excitement for being married to the love of my life, but the sorrow of leaving a lifetime of treasures behind in my family and friends caused meoverwhelming sadness.

As I shuffle now through my contacts on the smartphone, the memories of that day are but a shadow. God has sent me faithful friends through the years: Friends "who have picked me up when I fell down." Friends who have "kept me warm in cold valleys of my life." Indeed, Solomon must have thought of some of my friends when he wrote Ecclesiastes 4!

On the opposite spectrum of our list of bad influences, there is another list that needs to be highlighted as the mighty helpers in the construction of our Faith Bridge. They're our true friends.

We must identify them, lock them in our hearts, cherish and invest in our relationship with them. There is no doubt that true friendship is one of God's greatest gifts to us. As Solomon said, *"pity the man who falls and has no one to help him up!"*

Good friends tell you like it is, with love.

"Dear brothers and sisters, if another believer is overcome by some sin, you who are godly should gently and humbly help that person back onto the right path." Galatians 6:1a

I am blessed to have a couple of friends who will "tell it like it is" when I need to hear it. My friends Adriana and Terri in particular have become like strong compasses in my life. They're both women of prayer and wisdom and God has used them numerous times to point out flaws in my character that needed change. However (and this is so very important), they're also the first ones to encourage me and rejoice with me with every small milestone conquered. I treasure their honesty and reassurance.

True friends give sacrificially

> *"Greater love has no one than this, that someone lay down his life for his friends." John 15:13*

How many times have I needed a friend when it was inconvenient for them! If you live far from your family like I do, you have needed the help of a dear friend at some point in time.

Indeed, true friends lay down their lives ... sacrificially. They stop and put aside their own daily plans, for a friend in need. They withhold criticism to show compassion to a friend who stumbled. True friends are givers. And sacrifice is one of the greatest demonstrations of love.

Truly, the gift of friendship was one of God's best ideas. It was another way He chose to display His love for us. True friendship stands against time, distance and trials. You may not speak for several months and even not see each other for years. Yet, your love for each other and dedication never changes. Love is the center of true friendship ... and this we know: love is the greatest gift of all.

> *"Three things will last forever — faith, hope, and love — and the greatest of these is love." I Corinthians 13:13*

True friends rejoice with you in your victories.

True friends can be trusted.

True friends are a channel of blessing between God and mankind.

As we ponder about the influence of others in our lives and how they impact our Faith Bridge, we must ask the question: are your friends helping you keep your faith ... or are they stumbling blocks?

Only you know the answer.

The next question is: What are you going to do about it?

Chapter 5

When you curse your own life

The buzz of the city circled him, making him alert to the lives that passed by. He sat at the bottom of the steps of the court house, where he knew many regulars would stop and drop their change into the old tin can.

He could feel the warmth of the sun on that fall morning. "Cling." Someone dropped one coin. He reached into the can. His fingers recognized the quarter. He heard several steps, as giggly young women came by. Their chatter turned into a silent reverence as they read his sign. "Cling, cling". Several coins this time. He might have enough for a cup of coffee to break his fast.

One hour passed by without the sound of one single coin, when he heard the hurried steps of a woman, the sound of the high heels giving out her slender figure. She passed him and suddenly stopped, retracing her steps back to him. He heard her stop in front of him and she stooped. He was startled when he realized that she had picked up his sign and started writing something on it.

He reached out and touched her shoes, just as she gently put the sign back down.

What followed puzzled the old man. Suddenly, the noise of the hurried steps of pedestrians was muffled by the ongoing avalanche of coins. For what seemed to be an eternity, the coins did not stop falling into his can, as more and more people seemed to be emptying out their pockets. He reached out and touched the can, realizing that it had become full to the brim.

Astounded, he emptied it into his old bag.

Several hours later he heard the same familiar steps. The same young lady was back. She stopped in front of him and stooped down again. Just to confirm that his ears did not trick him, he reached out and again touched her shoes.

His eyes were moist as he fought back the tears.

"What did you do to my sign?" the old man asked the young lady.

She touched his arm and then patted his face.

"I wrote the same, but different words."

On the old cardboard sign, where one once read: "I'm blind, please help", new compelling words screamed compassion to the passersby:

"It's a beautiful day ... and I can't see it."

The story above is portrayed in a powerful video produced by an on line content specialist agency from the UK. The video is used to reinforce the life-changing power of our words.

"Change your words. Change your world," the company's slogan says.[1]

The blind man in the story was reaping meager blessings because his words did not move people's hearts.

I believe many times we find ourselves in a similar situation. God has bountiful blessings that He wants to give us, but our words reflect a heart that is either too timid to ask or too faithless to receive.

Our words often give out the strength of our faith. Therefore I believe God is very interested on what comes out of our mouths, for it usually is a reflection on how much we love and trust Him.

God chose to create life with His word. Likewise, He will one day destroy His enemies by the power of His word (2 Thessalonians 2:8).

*When He created the Heavens and the earth — He spoke
(Genesis 1:3).*

Before He became flesh, He was the Word (John 1:1.)

When He raised Lazarus from the grave — He spoke (John 11:43).

Words therefore, are a big deal for God. They are powerful weapons that can be used to bless us ... or condemn us and those around us. The power of our words can actually destroy one's spirit, incite defeat and even cause violence. Our words can also directly inflict deep emotional wounds in the lives of those around us.

We are the only creatures made by God who are able to use this amazing gift of human speech. Therefore it's not surprising that He gives our words such prophetic power over our lives.

And it's no wonder our words have the power to influence our destiny.

Small blessings ... That's what was asked

Years ago, I heard a sermon illustration about a man who died and went to heaven. Upon arrival, he was greeted by Peter. The apostle escorted him to a huge room, where boxes were stacked up as high as the ceiling. He noticed that the left-side shelves had small, plain boxes. They did not seem to be able to hold much inside. The boxes on the right side, however, were large and ornate. They would certainly be the type of boxes to hold the most elaborate and expensive gifts.

The man turned to Peter and asked, "What do the boxes on the left hold?"

Peter answered, "These were all the gifts you received on earth as you made your petitions to the Father, or as you opened your mouth to declare goodness, love and edification into your life and the lives of those around you.

"What about the large beautiful boxes? What do they hold?" the man asked.

"They are the gifts that were intended for your life," Peter said. "Beautiful, aren't they? Bountiful. Huge. Eternally rewarding. But they never left Heaven. You never asked. You never claimed them. Therefore, you never received them."

Indeed, I can't help but wonder how many gifts, originally intended for us, are left behind, unclaimed, just because we chose to be timid and did not ask.

Conversely, I wonder how many curses we bring into our lives by what we do say.

I truly believe that many of us cannot get victory over our circumstances and problems because the same mouths that praise God ... curse their fellow men ... or constantly declare defeat over their own lives.

"Does a spring of water bubble out with both fresh water and bitter water?"
James 3:11

"I praise you, God."
"I can't do anything right."
"God is so good."
"If it's bad, it will happen to me."

We often do not realize how much our words influence the course of our lives. The devil uses the words that we speak as tools of discouragement, which keep us from believing in the awesome power of God.

How many of us find ourselves sharing our burdens with our friends and family as if they were permanent?

How many times do we forget that, instead, the Bible promises that "our momentary, light affliction is producing for us an eternal weight of glory far beyond all comparison."[2] We carry on our self-destructing talk, speaking as if God has forgotten us and as if we were cursed, instead of blessed.

If you were to take inventory of our speech, would you say your tongue declares life ... or death?

Unfortunately, I'd say many of us speak more death than life into our lives. This may not necessarily be true about every aspect of one's life, but we all struggle with negative thoughts in one area or another, which are translated into negative words.

Speaking death into our finances

Finances may just be one of the worst things to be positive about at this day and age. Many people in the United States and the world have seen their life style change tremendously in the past decade or so. Unemployment is at an all-time high. Prices are up. Raises are down.

Many of us have had a time of financial struggle.

About nine years ago, my husband and I lost a substantial amount of money when we had to sell a business that we owned at a huge loss. It has taken us many years to be able to pay off and recover from that debt. During this time, we have also felt convicted to keep our children in Christian schools. Needless to say, money has been tight, to say the least.

Speaking financial blessings into our lives has become a true challenge.

But some time ago, God convicted me of this truth: If I believe God is indeed Jehovah, Jireh, our Provider, why would I insist on cursing our finances by declaring what we don't have, instead of what we do have?

Better yet, how can God bless us financially, if we act as if He were a stingy Father who has pleasure withholding good things from His children?

Don't get me wrong, I'm not talking about naming and claiming. I completely refute the type of theology that believes that, if you are going through financial problems, it's because your faith is not big enough. Nonsense! That's the same as believing that all sick people are ill because their faith is weak. That's an evil theology that disregards that God is in the process of making us and molding us into the image of Jesus. It is greatly through suffering that He fulfills this process.

On the other hand, however, if I believe my Bible to be true, then I have to take Proverbs 18:21 seriously. In other words, I cannot expect a financial blessing if I walk around talking constantly about my problems due to lack of money.

Instead, God calls me to praise Him regardless of my financial situation. He wants me to thank Him for all the blessings He pours into my life, instead of talking about the things that I don't have but think I deserve. And instead of complaining, or talking about what I lack, He calls me to declare my trust in Him through praying and thanksgiving.

He calls me to utter words of trust that move His heart:

"Rejoice in the Lord always; again I will say, rejoice!
Let your gentle spirit be known to all men. The Lord is near.
Be anxious for nothing, but in everything by prayer and
supplication with thanksgiving let your requests be made
known to God." Philippians 4:4-6

So the next time you feel tempted to speak death into your finances, hold your tongue. Choose to thank Him instead.

Speaking death into our health

"There is one whose rash words are like sword thrusts, but the tongue of the wise brings healing." Proverbs 12:18

A nurse friend told me a sad story about a patient who declared defeat over her life for many years and ended up reaping a deadly disease. This lady would come to my friend's office and declare: "I know I'll have cancer. I just know it."

My friend was puzzled because this lady had no family history of cancer and was a very healthy woman overall. But she would come to their office and always be negative about her health, seemingly trying to validate her "prophecy". Not long ago, her declaration turned into reality. She had cancer.

Is it possible that one could become sick because of the words they say? We cannot generally speaking affirm that, but I do take seriously the many times in Scriptures where God links our physical and emotional wellbeing with the words that come out of our mouths. While words cannot actually cause a severe or chronic disease such as diabetes or cancer, I believe the way we react to our conditions with our words and actions can be directly connected to the outcome of many illnesses. And if a person is affected by a mental or emotional disorder, this becomes especially true.

"Death and life are in the power of the tongue, and those who love it will eat its fruit." Proverbs 18:21

Yes, it is well to refute diseases and stop speaking about how bad we feel. Instead, we should thank God for His healing. "By His stripes we are healed!" Isaiah 53:5. Declare it. Because it is true. Whether in this life, or on the one to come, His healing is a promise. Praise Him for that and do not think that your condition is a negative payback from Him.

Speaking death into our jobs

> *"I hate my job."*
> *"I hate my boss."*
> *"I'll never get that promotion."*
> *"Is it 5 o'clock yet?"*

How can we thank God for His provision and yet curse the means which He uses to provide for us?

Isn't it the same as cursing God's provision for us?

Harsh? No.

Truth.

We bow our heads to thank God for our food, our homes, our cars. And yet the same mouth that thanks Him for those blessings, often curses the means He uses to provide them. If we believe that God is the One who gives us our jobs, why would we dare curse them? Or those who He has put above us?

> *"Every person is to be in subjection to the governing authorities. For there is no authority except from God, and those which exist are established by God. Therefore whoever resists authority has opposed the ordinance of God; and they who have opposed will receive condemnation upon themselves." Romans 13:1-6*

This verses remind us that all authority that has ever been in power, from presidents to dictators ... from your boss to your teacher ... they are where they are because God allowed them to be in power.

I know it's hard to believe that, when we see some of the

decisions we see in governments and companies. But it is the truth from the Word of God: No one is in power unless God establishes them. As Solomon said:

"The king's heart is like channels of water in the hand of the Lord; He turns it wherever He wishes." Proverbs 21:1

That truth should change the way we behave towards all authority. We may not like their decisions, but we must remember that God has not stepped down from the throne when He allowed certain politicians to be elected or your boss to take the job. Once you grasp that truth, you realize that there is nothing that men can do to harm you, unless God allows them. And if He does, there certainly is a reason for it.

God may just be working on your attitude.

Or on your gratitude.

He may be waiting on you to get to a point of total surrender and trust before He moves you from where you are.

But as long as you complain about your job, your hours, or your colleagues, you need to know that you are cursing the very provision God is sending your way.

I am here to tell you, by my own experience, that at the right time, God will remove you from under an unjust boss. He will not allow you to stay at that job even one day longer than necessary.

So, in the meantime, stop cursing your provision. Instead, pray for those who persecute you (Mathew 5:43-45). That's not a suggestion. It's the heart of the gospel of Jesus Christ. You'll be surprised of how God will bless you and how fast He will free you once you start obeying Him and praying for your enemies.

Believe me, I'm speaking from experience.

You don't need to defend yourself against your enemies. God is your justice. Don't ever forget that. With the Lord of the universe

at your side, whom shall you fear?
Speak out blessing!

    Jesus addressed the power of spoken faith on Mark 11:23-24: *"Truly I say to you, whoever **says** to this mountain, 'Be taken up and cast into the sea, and does not doubt in his heart, but believes that what he **says** is going to happen, it will be granted him. Therefore I say to you, all things for which you **pray and ask,** believe that you have received them, and they will be granted you."*

    Notice that Jesus is addressing faith that is conveyed in words. Four times did Jesus use verbs that required a declaration of faith. It is not enough to believe in our hearts. We must declare. We must declare, with our tongues, that what we believe will happen. That mountain will not move until we **speak** in faith.

    Moses also addressed the choices we make with our tongues when he said to Israel:

"But the word is very near you, in your mouth and in your heart, that you may observe it. See, I have set before you today life and prosperity, and death and adversity." Deuteronomy 30:14-15.

    Notice that Moses said these words as a prophetic admonition to Israel, a little before his death, when he was preparing to pass the baton of leadership to Joshua. He gave Israel two options: (1) To serve God in righteousness and therefore have a prosperous life or (2) To disobey God and therefore reap disaster and death.

    It's interesting that Moses said that the key to these two options was in the people's hearts and **tongues.** It would be in their hearts, because that's where they would decide whether or not to act on what they believed.

But everything would be sealed with their tongue.

Moses was saying that God's people would seal what they truly believed with their words, and therefore bring either life and prosperity, or death and adversity.

That same principle is still alive today. You can choose to believe God at His Word, thus receiving victory over your finances, health and relationships. Or you can choose to keep talking about your problems as if God is not able to provide, protect and heal.

A testimony issue

Jeryn was your typical 9-year old: lively, fun and with enough energy to get three of me going for an entire day. As she sat around while her mom and I talked, I would never imagine that she paid attention to what I do or don't do or to what inspires me.

Therefore I was surprised when she handed me a small gift bag containing her personal gift for my birthday a couple of years ago. Inside it, I found something she had picked herself: a beautiful, tiny sculpture of a flying eagle coming back to her nest, where eaglets anxiously waited for their food.

My little friend looked up at me, her face beaming with pride of her finding. Her mom then told me that she found the sculpture in a garage sale and thought of me. She used her own money to buy the gift. Needless to say, her gift blessed my heart. But I honestly was taken by surprise that little Jeryn — busy-hopping-around Jeryn — had paid attention long enough to know that her mom's friend loves eagles so much.

Yes — little Jeryn may have been busy playing hide and seek with my children, but she was certainly aware.

And so are my two little girls.

And so are your children, grandchildren, nieces and nephews.

Their little eyes and ears are watching. And their little feet are eager to follow you.

In Deuteronomy 11, Moses instructed God's people to obey God's laws. He emphasized the importance of teaching them to their children. And although it seems like he was only talking about speaking truth and teaching God's principles, I believe he meant much more than that. He encouraged the Israelites to teach them as they sat around their homes, from sun dawn to sun set and as they went by doing their daily routines. In other words, he was also admonishing them to live what they preached.

"Do what I say, but don't do as I do"

I know that there are exceptions to this, but I believe that, for the most part, one of the reasons so many teenagers and young adults who were raised in church later rebel against God, is because they lived in a home filled with hypocrisy.

I have heard that from so many people and have witnessed it in lives around me. Many of us, who go to church every week and are highly involved in ministry, are not always teaching God's principles with our words and actions at home.

Of course, we all do it to a certain degree, because we are human. Therefore at times you and I will fail to present a godly character to our children and other people in our lives. Life gets tough some days and we may be too tired or too worried about things that are happening and find ourselves having a bad attitude. If one is a human, that is normal, as long as these attitudes are the exception, not the rule.

On days like that, we must remember that we have God's grace. We must repent, then, ask the person whom we hurt to forgive us (yes, even if it's your 3 year old), learn the lesson and move on.

The problem is when our entire lives are the opposite of what we preach. If you make your children quote and memorize the fruit of the spirit in Galatians 5, but on that same day they witness you lose your temper with their daddy over something small (for the fifth time that week), guess which lesson they learned?

Yep. Not joy, peace, gentleness, patience, love, goodness and self-control!

They just learned that mommy cannot control her tongue ... and does not cultivate the fruit of the spirit in her life.

You just taught them a lesson on how to curse their relationships.

If you go to church and shout praises to the King, lifting your hands in worship, and then you come home and yell at them for the smallest thing, guess what little Sally will think, who was standing right beside you during worship?

Well, for one, you just taught her that it's ok not to live by what she learns at Sunday school.

If you are at church each time the door is open, have time to take on one more responsibility in the name of Jesus, but have no time to listen to your preteen share her struggles at school, I can almost guarantee you that she will resent church and possibly God Himself.

The truth is — as Moses instructed God's people on how to teach God's statures to their children, he made it a point that they should teach them with their lives, not only with their words. If we live what we preach, if we strive to follow God with all our might, not to impress people, but to lead them to the Savior, the first ones who will want to follow us are the little ones in our lives.

They will see the joy, peace and contentment that we display and their feet will be eager to follow us. And as they do, the promises of God will follow the next generation, just as He has promised the Israelites:

"(...) so that your days and the days of your sons may be multiplied on the land which the Lord swore to your fathers to give them, as long as the heavens remain above the earth. For if you are careful to keep

71

all this commandment which I am commanding you to do, to love the Lord your God, to walk in all His ways and hold fast to Him, then the Lord will drive out all these nations from before you, and you will dispossess nations greater and mightier than you. Every place on which the sole of your foot treads shall be yours (...)"
Deuteronomy 11:21-24

My prayer is that we will hold fast to the truth that no matter how much we proclaim the gospel, if we are not allowing our lives to be transformed by its power, we are failing.

Moreover, if we serve God in whatever ministry God has called us to do, but are pushing the people in our lives away from Him because of the discrepancy between our speech and our lives, we have certainly failed.

Our ministry is first at home with our families and very particularly, with our children. It should start with what we declare with our mouths and follow with lives that glorify Him in deeds and fruit.

Bottom Line

In the process of identifying issues that are keeping our Faith Bridge broken, we must take an honest inventory of what comes out of our mouths, as well as how we live out our faith.

We cannot claim to trust God and declare death into our lives.

We cannot have a strong faith-walk connection unless our mouths declare that which we know about our God.

Regardless of our circumstances, we must fix our eyes on the unseen blessings that are ready to be poured down over us. We must remember the vision of those large, blingy boxes that He has for us in heaven, ready to bless our lives with "more than we can ask or pray for"(Ephesians 3:20).

Likewise, we must ask God to show us if there is anything in our attitude that is directly opposite of what we preach with our tongue. If and when He shows us, we must make an effort to pay attention to our actions and change them so that our walk matches our talk.

We must also make a special effort to be more aware that the people in your life (and especially children) are all ears and eyes and are constantly watching us. Ask God to help you be a godly example that will help them want to follow Jesus.

There is incredible power in the tongue. Were it not so, God would not have chosen words to give life and make light out of darkness. We must realize that truth and make a conscious effort to avoid words that curse our lives and the lives of those around us. It's not an easy process, mainly if you've been using negative words all your life. But if we are to maintain a strong Twelve-Inch Faith Bridge, the words that come out of your mouth can be used as tools to build it ... or destroy it.

The choice is on the tip of your tongue.

Chapter 6

Spending Time with the Architect

In the first part of this book, I exposed the issues that keep us from developing and maintaining a good connection between our emotions and our faith walk. Indeed, as we allow our actions, thoughts, words and the deeds that drive these to interfere with the truths that we know about our God, we cannot navigate life's high and lows without losing sight … and often losing faith.

That's the reason why so many people give up on God when facing difficult trials. Or why those who allow the world's views to contaminate their thoughts and actions end up distancing themselves from the God whom they knew earlier in life.

I pray that the first part of this book has helped you identify your personal issues — your own "red flags". It is my hope and prayer that you can eliminate those things which are contributing to the instability of your faith and that this book will guide you in pursuing the things that will help strengthen it.

I don't intend to leave you alone.

Please understand that I come to you with a humble heart.

A heart that has been tried and tested; a heart that has proven that those issues that I mentioned on the previous chapters indeed weigh down our Faith Bridge.

The purpose of the second part of this book is to help you identify those steps that you can take in order to build and maintain a strong Faith Bridge. This is where we will start following the steps that you will need in order to *"bridge the gap between how you feel and what you know about your God."*

Whether you're young in the faith, or a seasoned Christian, it really doesn't matter. We all have emotions and we all have challenges in life that can potentially help deteriorate our relationship with God.

But I'm here to tell you that God does not mean for the problems we face to destroy our relationship with Him. His objective when allowing these trials is to strengthen it.

But you must understand- because of the free will He gives, the choice between allowing the problems you face to destroy your love for God — or strengthen it — is not God's.

It is yours.

I speak from experience.

I've gone through cancer, long-term unemployment, a huge business loss, a tragic death in our family.

These trials have not made bitter. I believe they have made me better.

Why is it, you ask?

Is Patricia a super-Christian?

No. Far from it. I just made some crucial, deliberate choices. I chose to seek God, not flee from Him. Therefore these trials accomplished what God designed them to accomplish: strengthen my faith, love and devotion to Him.

I have not lost my faith. Rather, I believe it's stronger than ever. I have also watched faithful, godly people in my life go through terrible valleys. Indeed, I've watched family members and close friends go through what some would call "hell on earth" and yet, never curse God.

Instead, just like Job, we have all chosen to say:

"The Lord gave and the Lord has taken away. Blessed be the name of the Lord." Job 1:21

Therefore the intention of this second part is to tell you: "Come, my friend. Let me show you what I have learned. I may not know exactly how you feel, but I know what it is to be faced with challenges that are bigger than what you think you can handle. Let me tell you what I have learned. Hold my hand. With God's help and by His grace, let's build your Twelve-Inch Faith Bridge."

First Things First

The first thing I have to tell you is that I don't believe in self-help. My "self" only gets me in trouble.

I need the help of the Trinity — Father, Son and Holy Spirit. That's what I need.

You need it, too.

The number one item as we start building our Twelve-Inch Faith Bridge is to evaluate our prayer life.

I call it "Spending Time with the Architect."

God holds the blueprint to help you build your Faith Bridge and He is longing to reveal it to you, but you must seek Him first.

If your prayer life is mediocre or non-existent, your soul is hungry. If your soul is hungry, it will seek to fill the void with something other than God. No question about it.

There is a hole in man's heart that only God can fill. In 1670, Blaise Pascal introduced this concept in his book "Pensées,"[1] written as a defense of Christianity. The concept of the "God-shaped hole," however, has taken on a life of its own and has been used by various theist authors to refer to that perpetual thirst in man's soul that only God is able to quench.

Many spend their lives attempting to fill that void with possessions, food, relationships or accomplishments, and often get to the end of their lives feeling hopeless and defeated.

On the other hand, we meet people of great faith who have very few possessions and even go through unimaginable pain without losing joy and hope.

In her best-selling book, *Made to Crave,* Lysa Terkeurst talks about this longing for God that every soul has, and all along is intended to bring us to a deep, intimate relationship with our Maker. She says:

"Indeed, our souls are thirsty and ravenous vacuums. If we fail to understand how to fill our souls with spiritual nourishment, we will forever be triggered to numb our longings with other temporary physical pleasures."[2]

The only way out of this undernourished, starving cycle is to put God where He belongs: in that God-shaped hole inside your heart.

Guess what? You can only know someone, if you spend time with him or her.

Duh, right? This is a no brainer.

Your must seek to know God

"And they who know Your name [who have experience and acquaintance with Your mercy] will lean on and confidently put their trust in You. And they who know Your name [who have experience and acquaintance with Your mercy] will lean on and confidently put their trust in You, for You, Lord, have not forsaken those who seek (inquire of and for) You [on the authority of God's Word and the right of their necessity]." Psalm 9:9-10 (Amplified Bible)

According to the Eerdmans Bible dictionary, the Hebrew word for "know" in the original text means: to understand, to grasp or ascertain; especially to be familiar or acquainted with a person or thing.

Psalm 9 is a song of praise — a call to worship from David. In this Psalm he recalls how God has empowered him to triumph over the Philistines and other neighboring nations that fought against his throne (2 Samuel 5:8.)

This is not a first-timer, new believer song of praise. It's the song from a heart that searched God and found Him during the trials of life. It's the song of praise of one who has tested and proved God the Deliverer, Redeemer and Strong Tower, a Present Help in times of trouble.

I love the second part of verse 10. It gives hope to those who are yet to find true, intimate relationship with God:

"For You, LORD, have not forsaken those who seek You."

David reminds us that God's grace and presence is extended to all who seek Him. Thanks to the new covenant established by Jesus on the cross, all who have trusted Him as their Savior can seek God and find Him in the most intimate way.

Do You See Him As The Man Upstairs ... Or as your Eternal Daddy?

The front door opened and I heard four little feet running to it. "Daaaaaaadyyyy!" I smile as I hear the sounds of kisses and giggles. I turn around and my heart takes a leap. The three people I love most on earth are all smiles.

It does not matter how hard the day was anymore.

Problems with friends at school? Difficult homework?

In a moment, they just know it - all is fine, for daddy is home.

I reflect back on my childhood and how I was absolutely crazy about my daddy (I still am). He was Superman!! He knew it all. He could do anything. He was also the strongest, smartest, richest and most handsome man alive. If you were blessed by being raised by a loving dad, you know what I am talking about.

If you asked us, daddy's girls, we would not have any problem believing that our dads hung the moon.

Because we really believe they could.

The word "Abba" as a reference to God is an Aramaic word which literally means "daddy" or "papa".

Jesus cried out to His Daddy in the garden of Gethsemane, at a time of great distress, when He was about to give Himself as a ransom for mankind's sins (Matt 14:36). The apostle Paul also used the expression "Abba, Father," when referring to the fact that we were adopted by God when we accepted Christ as our Savior, and therefore we may boldly claim our heritage as children of the Mighty God of Israel:

"So you have not received a spirit that makes you fearful slaves. Instead, you received God's Spirit when he adopted you as his own children. Now we call him, 'Abba, Father.'" (Romans 8:15 — NLT)

Many of us have different names by which people call us.

If someone calls me "Mrs. Holbrook", unless they are thirteen years old or under, the verdict is simple — they just don't know me. On the other hand, different nicknames and loving abbreviations are normally a demonstration of how close someone is to me.

I have this habit for as long as I remember: if you are part of my family or a close friend, I normally have a nickname for you. It's usually one which most people you know don't use for you. When someone changes from an acquaintance to a friend, most likely, they will receive a special nickname from me.

It's not something planned, it just happens and I know exactly why. The more I get to know someone, the more I love them, the more intimate we become. You are not just someone that I see and wave to as you pass by. You become special to me and so I give you a special name. You know me better than many people.

I call you friend and that's important to me.

Indeed, intimate and true relationships are hard to find. There is a reason for that - it takes time to develop them.

You cannot expect to be close to someone unless you spend time with them, unselfishly giving yourself to them … unless you are willing to put your own interests aside for them.

Likewise, in many aspects, true and intimate earthly relationships mirror the connection we should have with our Heavenly Father.

We should know Him - as a child that covers her father's face with kisses as she sits on his lap, uninvited, simply because she knows him.

We should know Him — as my husband and I know each other.

We can look at each other across a room full of people and know what the other one is thinking. We trust each other because we know each other. Likewise, the more intimately we know God, the more we learn to trust Him.

And we become intimate with God through prayer and by studying His Word.

Define prayer, please.

You may be thinking — *"Cool. I got that. I pray. What's next?"*

Let me tell you that I thought I knew how to pray until God revealed the truth about my prayer life about nine years ago. I was used to worship and prayer until I realized that my prayer life was suffering from A.D.H.D.

Bear with me. I bet you can relate.

I was home with one small child and pregnant with our second daughter, as busy as a pregnant mother of a toddler can be. I would start praying and a thought would cross my mind and, I would quickly move my attention from God to whatever was on my mind.

I could sense that my prayers would go up the room, hit the ceiling and bounce back down.

Reading God's Word was no different. I would start reading something and would get lost in my thoughts and preoccupations for the day. Quickly and steadily, my prayer life became dull and God became this distant Creator, whom I reverenced and respected, but whom I could not, in all honesty, relate to as a Father.

Can you relate? I believe that all Christians go through a phase such as this at some point in time. We allow the cares of this world to distract us. Or, worse yet, our fellowship with the Father is broken because of deliberate, known sin in our lives.

A lack of intimacy with God is never, ever, the Father's fault. It is ours. And if you have a hard time concentrating and being quiet before Him, you may need to do what I did.

You may have to get into the closet.

For years I have heard my pastor Dr. Charles Stanley talking about his experience praying in the closet. He has a place in his house and ministry - a dark room with nothing but a pillow and his Bible, where he retires to be alone with God.

So, some time ago, when my family was visiting from Brazil, I could not find a place to pray. I decided to arrange my own prayer closet in the house - a place where God and I could meet in the dark.

A place of silence, nothingness even, where I quietly wait on God to speak. And so I rearranged my walk-in closet and embarked on this amazing journey that changed my prayer life.

As I settle in the dark closet, I ask Him what to do that day. More than praying, I am there to have communion with Him, to bask in His presence.

In the silence of that closet, God admonishes me, directs me and loves on me.

The closet has become the "Abba and me" place. Daddy and His girl.

Priceless. Soul-changing.

But I have to say, I don't always pray in the closet.

And it may even not be an option for you.

There were times where my "closet" was my car, during my commute hours in Atlanta traffic.

Or my walk in the park.

The point is not where, but what.

We have such crazy-busy lives nowadays, that unless we give Him silence, we can easily miss His voice.

He speaks. ALL! THE! TIME! But are we listening? The reason why many of us end up "slipping" into a life of spiritual complacency is because we do not hear our Lord.

Truly, as Abba's children, we really should not need a pastor or a friend to tell us how to live. We should be able to hear Him ourselves … and then, simply obey.

Before anything else, we need to allow God to change US. We need to be still for long enough to allow Him to show us His to do list for our days.

Don't have time, huh?

Well, if you have time to watch the next episode of that reality show, you have time for a conversation with God.

If you have time to exercise in the park, that's a perfect time to commune with Him. Take your "closet" with you to the park!

Want a strong Twelve-Inch Faith Bridge?

Consult with the Architect. He knows the drawings. He knows your weaknesses. He knows your blueprint.

Spend time with the Master Architect of your life's plan. He can't wait to show you His amazing plan...

And His ways...

And His promises...

Sit still in Abba's wonderful Presence. And get ready to be blessed.

But how do I pray?

"Now it came to pass, as He was praying in a certain place, when He ceased, that one of His disciples said to Him, "Lord, teach us to pray, as John also taught his disciples." (Luke 11:1 - NKJV)

A story is told about the great English Christian poet and philosopher Samuel Taylor Coleridge in his biography:

"It was shortly before Coleridge's death and he was talking to his biographer about the Lord's Prayer in Luke 11. He said: I have no difficulty as to forgiveness (...) Neither do I find or reckon the most solemn faith in God as a real object the most arduous act of the reason or will. Oh, no, my dear, it is to pray — to pray as God would have us: this is what at times makes me turn cold to my soul. Believe me, to pray with all your heart and strength, with the reason and will, to believe vividly that God will listen to your voice through Christ, and verily do the thing He pleases thereupon — this is the last, the greatest achievement of the Christian's warfare on earth. Teach us to pray, oh, Lord!" [3]

I have been reciting the Lord's Prayer for as long as I can remember. Having been raised in a Catholic school, it was part of each morning's ritual.

When I got saved at age 25, I remember thinking: *"Why would the Lord teach us such a simple prayer?"* No big words, no long sentences.

The Lord's Prayer was simply not fancy enough.

Then I studied it closer. And as I started peeling off the layers of what was under the simple words He taught us and as I went on reading the parable in verses 5-13 of Luke 11, I realized that this simple Prayer reveals the essence of our relationship with God: Our worship, His forgiveness, His provision, His protection, His faithfulness and our trust.

In this passage, Jesus presents this prayer as a brief but comprehensive summary of the desires of a true disciple of Christ.

"Our Father in Heaven, Hallowed be Your name.

Your kingdom come.

Your will be done.

On earth, as it is in Heaven." (NKJV)

The Lord's Prayer points us to the essence of what we should seek in our prayer time:

Petition #1: His Glory and the progress of His Kingdom should be the first focus of our lives:

The fact that the prayer starts by praising God and continues with petitions for the progress of God's kingdom is very significant in many ways.

It rebukes our selfishness and frames our minds and hearts to make our first and deepest desire that God's kingdom be advanced and His name glorified on earth.

Furthermore, it validates what God spelled out on the first three commandments of the Mosaic Law: God is to be the main focus of our lives; His will and progress of His kingdom should be our first desire.

Also, when we ask that His will be done, we get positioned to accept God's will for our lives, no matter at what cost. His paths many times lead us to trials, but if we see our lives as a key piece in His kingdom around us, we will totally change the way we see our trials.

Can you count the times that you have gone through a valley, just to see, months or years later, that you have been positioned to help someone who is facing exactly what you went through? I know I have!

How could you be equipped had you not walked in their shoes? How could your testimony be really effective?

Exactly. Your personal testimony validates your right to even offer comfort to those going through the valley.

Petition #2: Provide for the needs of my body and my soul:
"Give us day by day our daily bread."

Not only should we ask God for our daily provision, but we should also request His divine favor in spiritual matters.

"Hawvlan lachma d'sunganan yaomana"

(Give us this day our daily bread, in Aramaic)

In Aramaic, the word bread means more than just the bread we eat. The word "bread" *(lachma)* is related to the word "wisdom" *(hochma)*. Therefore Jesus herein connects the bread that our bodies need to the spiritual bread that our souls long for.

Without material provision, our bodies would perish. Likewise, without spiritual food, our souls would perish. God wants us to have both. We need *hochma* to thrive spiritually and *lachma* to thrive physically.

For a child of God, the first is even more essential than the latter.

Petition #3: Forgive us … but first, teach us how to forgive
"And forgive us our sins; for we also forgive everyone that is indebted to us."

Forgiveness of our sins is usually one of the main reasons we first come to Christ. We realize our sinful nature and understand why He went to Calvary. We then confess our sin and happily accept His gift of forgiveness by grace, the ultimate reason for how and why we obtain the gift of eternal life.

However, we must remember that God's forgiveness does not exclude us from the obligation to forgive others. We often go on our merry ways, our sins forgiven but many times withholding forgiveness for those who hurt us.

That's when we hurt the heart of the One who paid the ultimate sacrifice for our complete forgiveness.

What right do we have to withhold forgiveness when He forgave us all?

How can the Lord hear our prayers if we are holding grudges in our hearts?

I know the answer. He cannot.

We may fool ourselves saying that the Lord is near, listening and blessing us when our hearts are dark with unforgiveness and bitterness. But make no mistake; He will only hear us until we realize the sin of unforgiveness that haunts us and set the person who wronged us free.

God cannot dwell in darkness, and an unforgiving spirit is one that denies the very reason we have His favor in the first place.

Want God to listen to your prayers?

Then forgive as you have been forgiven.

Petition #4: Keep my feet from falling, oh Lord!

"And do not lead us into temptation, but deliver us from the evil one."

We are all going to be tempted by Satan. He's been around for much longer than any of us. He knows all of man's ways and he knows exactly how to get to us.

The fact that the Lord emphasizes in His prayer that we are to ask Him to keep us from evil should give us encouragement. We are NOT alone! I'm reminded of 1 Corinthians 10:13:

"No temptation has overtaken you except such as is common to man; but God is faithful, who will not allow you to be tempted beyond what you are able, but with the temptation will also make the way to escape, that you may be able to bear it."

If there is anything in our lives that has the potential to become a stronghold for Satan, we need to lay it down. We need to willingly walk in the opposite direction of any door leading to the path that will make us fall.

Whatever our weaknesses, we should never underestimate either our enemy or our flesh. We cannot defeat either alone.

On the other hand, the Lord has promised He would help us keep our feet from falling and He instructs us to ask Him to do so. However, we should shun any path that leads us into where we know we will fall.

For how can we ask God "Lead us not" there, when we deliberately walk into it?

The Lord's Prayer is quite simple, but its purpose is not shallow. Its meaning when carefully studied opens the door to a sincere and fruitful prayer life. Its content covers each one of the steps for a close relationship with God. Should we follow the Lord's instructions, we should indeed accomplish the ultimate goal of the Christian life on earth — to glorify our Heavenly Father.

And in the process, as we hear from the One who created us, we should indeed find the abundant life that He promised us (John 10:10).

Persistence in prayer

When I was a little girl, I waited for a very special gift for many years.

I was about six years old when I started asking my dad for a piano. I started playing it when I was just five and it quickly became a passion. I would go to piano lessons twice every week. I loved it!

For many years, my piano was just a dream, as I'd practice day in and day out on an imaginary keyboard on our dining room table.

On birthdays, Christmas and any other special occasion there might be, I had only one request: I wanted my piano.

I remember the disappointment when each Christmas would come and go and I did not have my biggest dream fulfilled.

Then one cold winter evening in 1981, I was home when my parents arrived from work. We had dinner and after that, Dad said he thought someone was knocking at the front door. As I went to the foyer to open the door, right there, before my eyes, set a beautiful piano.

My seven-year-old dream had finally come true.

With tears of joy, I sat on my piano and played it for the first time. I woke up in the middle of the night and checked to make sure it was still there.

After a long time knocking at my dad's door, asking for the same gift repeatedly, he gave me the desire of my heart.

As a child, waiting was no fun. And it still is painful. I don't think that will ever change. What has changed, however, is my understanding on why I have to wait.

There are several reasons as to why God delays answering our prayers. We must realize that waiting is one of God's best teaching processes.

After the Lord's Prayer on Luke 11, Jesus told a parable that teaches us that we should never faint when it comes to praying for our heart's desire:

"Then He said to them, "Suppose one of you has a friend, and goes to him at midnight and says to him, 'Friend, lend me three loaves; for a friend of mine has come to me from a journey, and I have nothing to set before him'; and from inside he answers and says, 'Do not bother me; the door has already been shut and my children and I are in bed; I cannot get up and give you anything.' I tell you, even though he will not get up and give him anything because he is his friend, yet because of his persistence he will get up and give him as much as he needs. So I say to you, ask, and it will be given to you; seek, and you will find; knock, and it will be opened to you. For everyone who asks, receives; and he who seeks, finds; and to him who knocks, it will be opened. Now suppose one of you fathers is asked by his son for a fish; he will not give him a snake instead of a fish, will he?" Luke 11:5-11

Jesus was teaching perseverance in prayer. I would like to point out two lessons to be learned from this passage in Scriptures.

Lesson #1: No discouragements are ever to stop us from praying:

It is very insightful to realize that in this passage, the traveler is very demanding and his friend is very selfish. He is lying in bed at night, when the traveler knocks asking for help. He does not get up. He tells his friend to go away.

It's pretty obvious that Jesus is making a very strong contrast in order to make a point: Even the most selfish people will eventually hear us if we only keep on knocking.

God, in great contrast, not only in comparison to a friend of the traveler, but in comparison to an earthly father, will surely not ignore our plea.

"Yet, because of his persistence, he will get up and give him
as much as he needs." (v. 8b).

These words of the Lord are not to be interpreted as if God is reluctant to answer our prayers, and therefore we must seek Him with more energy and pray louder as the worshippers of Baal seemed to believe to be the case (1 Kings 18). Rather, we should think of God as our Loving Father, who, for our sake, delays His answer that we may be more disciplined in devotion to Him.

He often delays the answer that we may learn how to worship the Giver and not the gift.

But there is another hidden lesson about our prayer requests that we must understand:

Lesson # 2: Our prayers must pass through God's grid:

This is pretty basic, but nonetheless important.

We can forget about receiving a positive answer from God if our request does not meet His standards of righteousness, if our request goes against His principles, or if the timing is wrong.

We must ask ourselves if what we are asking passes a simple test: Does it glorify Him? Does it honor His word?

I believe we can easily meet these criteria if we just use Philippians 4:8 as we honestly evaluate our desires:

"Finally, brethren, whatever is true, whatever is honorable, whatever is right, whatever is pure, whatever is lovely, whatever is of good repute, if there is any excellence and if anything worthy of praise, dwell on these things."

Ok, then, if God is more loving and giving than any earthly Father could ever be, then why on earth do we have to wait, even when what we ask for passes through God's grid of what is honorable, right, pure, lovely and of good repute?

What's the meaning of God's silence?

I believe there are several reasons as to why God sometimes seems to be far away when we pray over and over again for the same good thing:

Reason # 1: As we keep on pleading, we draw closer to Him:

One of the reasons God delays His answers is because in the process of praying and waiting, our relationship with the Heavenly Father is strengthen and we receive new insights into His Spirit.

God will sometimes withhold His gifts that we may learn to desire greater things. He switches our minds and hearts to that which has eternal value.

It is significant that the Lord tells His disciples in this passage that if they knocked, if they asked, God would give them the Holy Spirit.

That is God's ultimate desire for all His disciples — that we should understand His ways and walk with Him in a deeper spiritual level. If He granted everything we ever asked for as soon as we asked for it, we would have no need to draw near Him and therefore would not know Him as He so wants us to.

Reason # 2: We may be asking for the wrong thing:

Even if our prayer request does pass God's grid as I mentioned earlier, even then, it may not be the right thing for YOU:

"All things are lawful for me, but not all things are profitable."
I Co 6:12 (NASB).

We may simply be asking for something that will give us temporary relief, whereas God has something much better in store for us than what we are asking for.

Reason # 3: It may just not be the right time yet:

Sometimes I imagine God looking down from Heaven and seeing all that is happening in the world at the same time.

"It is He who sits above the circle of the earth,
And its inhabitants are like grasshoppers ... " Isaiah 40:22a

He sees all the pieces of my life's puzzle and some pieces are not quite ready to be put in place. Some pieces are being worked on; they are being polished and improved.

He can see past, present and NOW is simply not the right time. I have to trust His plan and remember that if I want to be successful God's way, I need to "walk by faith, not by sight" 2 Co 5:7

A good example in my own life is regarding my husband. I had to wait until I was thirty years old to get married.

I was very busy with my own life until I was about 27 and then ... well, all my friends were married. Let me tell you: I was not happy to have to wait. But now as I look back, I clearly see it: I was not ready to be the wife God wanted me to be before.

It's a joke between my husband and me: had we met each other earlier; we probably would not have given each other a second thought. God had to work on both of us — and work He did! I am so very grateful today that I waited.

While I waited, Jesus became my all in many lonely moments and therefore we became close friends. And in His perfect time, He gave me the desire of my heart in the husband He chose for me.

Reason # 4: We may be expecting the answer in the wrong way:

Remember the story of Naaman on 2 Kings 5?

When Naaman asked the prophet Elisha to heal him, he thought Elisha would have an elaborate ceremony, evoking the powers of the

God of Israel as he laid hands on him as he was healed from leprosy. It seems as if expected something dramatic — dry ice, thunder and fireworks! To his disappointment, God's instructions to the prophet were simple: "Tell him to wash in the Jordan seven times."

Voila! Healed.

"That's it?" thought Naanman. "That's just too simple for me."

We may have already laid down the precise way God should heal or help us, and it may be that just as God did to Naaman, that He will respond in a different, perhaps a simpler way.

There may be an underlying issue in the way we respond to the simpler things: we may just think His open door is unworthy of us and therefore God may just be trying to teach us a lesson in humility or show us a new facet of His grace. I believe that was the lesson to Naaman.

It could also be yours.

The reward is not for the weak at heart:

We know by Jesus' teaching on this passage that while the friend did not respond immediately, he did grant the traveler's request.

And so it is with our Friend: He may not answer right away. It may take years for a specific prayer to be answered. He knows that if we receive all we ask at once, we should become overconfident and need Him no more.

But take heart, my friend: sooner or later and perhaps when you least expect it, our Heavenly Father, whose gifts are eternally good, will reward your persevering prayers with true blessings. We must ask and continually ask. We must knock and keep on knocking at the door of His mercy and power and He will surely open it to us.

When you feel like giving up … when you don't see God's answer coming, remember David's words in Psalms 37:25:

"I have been young and now I am old, yet I have not seen the righteous forsaken or his descendants begging bread." (NASB)

Remember this — your intercessor before the throne, Jesus Christ, understands exactly what you are going through.

Jesus Understands

My head was stuck to the pillow that morning. Any hope for energy had vanished with the dawn of a new day.

The sanguine in me wanted to jump out of bed and start the day as usual — study my Bible, prepare the kids for school, get ready, run out of the house to face Atlanta traffic.

But my body answered quickly: "No, ma'am. Not today. We're not getting up."

As I lay in bed, half conscious, I started muttering a prayer: "Jesus ... I need you to be the wind beneath my wings."

In the quietness of the moment, when a prayer is said and an answer is anticipated, I heard His tender voice whisper to my soul: "I've been there."

It seemed like a strange answer to me. I was hoping to hear something more like: *"Get up, take thy bed and walk!"* But His answer was clear: "I've been there."

"This High Priest of ours understands our weaknesses, for he faced all of the same testings we do (...)." Hebrews 4:15 (NLT)

Suddenly, images from Jesus' life on earth came to my mind — moments depicted in epic movies such as the *Passion of the Christ* and *Jesus* — the painful, unforgettable images of my Savior, as He suffered on his flesh more than any man or woman ever has or ever will.

I understood what He meant.

Jesus is as human as humans can be. He understands stress. And He certainly understands pain like no one else.

I did make it out of bed that day ... eventually.

As I opened my Bible the next day to continue my study on Hebrews, the Lord's answer from the day before still resounded on my mind. As I read the end of Chapter 4, God's answer to me started to make sense when I read the author's comments to His countrymen regarding the nature of our High Priest.

The book of Hebrews was written for the first century Messianic Jews. These men and women perfectly understood the establishment of priesthood. They knew that the high priests of the Old Testament had to be men appointed by God and consecrated for Him. After Christ's death and resurrection, there are no mentions to the title high priest" in the New Testament in reference to ministers within the church.

This title became Christ's alone. His atoning sacrifice on Calvary ended once and for all the Jewish priesthood, demonstrating that priests or animal sacrifices are no longer required.

Jesus — our Sympathetic High Priest

"Surely He has borne our griefs (sicknesses, weaknesses, and distresses) and carried our sorrows and pains [of punishment], yet we [ignorantly] considered Him stricken, smitten, and afflicted by God [as if with leprosy]. But He was wounded for our transgressions, He was bruised for our guilt and iniquities; the chastisement [needful to obtain] peace and well-being for us was upon Him, and with the stripes [that wounded] Him we are healed and made whole."
Isaiah 53:4-6 (Amplified)

The power of sympathy of our Great High Priest is not referred to as something that would distinguish Him from other high priests, but rather to express the resemblance and understanding that our Savior has regarding the feelings and struggles we all face.

"For He understands our weaknesses, for He faced all the same testings we do" (v.15)

The Greek word *astheneia* (transliteration) translated as "weaknesses" or "infirmities" in most texts, refers to both bodily infirmities, such as disease, as well as the general weaknesses of the human nature.

Jesus has suffered all our infirmities, both physically and emotionally. If it were not so, our King would not have been the Perfect Mediator between us and Holy God, for He would not be able to sympathize with our shortcomings and hurts.

You see, our Savior's unparalleled greatness as God, the Son, does not by any means make Him incapable of sympathy.

Although He is indeed the Son of God, He has a human soul — a soul actually, intensely human — which went through a complete array of trials and tribulations and reached Its glory through suffering.

Although He was without sin, He lived a life of constant temptation and sorrow because of the sin that assails mankind.

Therefore we understand the meaning of the prophetic voice of Isaiah as He foretold of our Great High Priest that He would "bear our griefs" — of sickness, disloyalty, irritations, loneliness and death. He knows, in His flesh, the precise force of every evil that ever tried and tempted mankind.

All things considered

"For since He Himself was tempted in that which He has suffered, He is able to come to the aid of those who are tempted." (Hebrews 2:18)

So, say you are facing a trial. A very difficult one.
Illness …
Stress…
Financial need …
Loneliness …
Overwhelming temptation…
Betrayal …
Death …

> *"Come to Me, all who are weary and heavy-laden,
> and I will give you rest." Matthew 11:28*

Go to the Architect, your High Priest. He's been there!

No matter where you look and what you are facing, there's not a facet of our humanity that Jesus did not experience.

Except sin.

He has gone through everything you and I experience and conquered every single temptation and overcame every single pain. Therefore you and I can boldly come and ask the Father, in the Son's Name and have the perfect confidence that He hears AND understands.

> *"So let us come boldly to the throne of our gracious God.
> There we will receive his mercy, and we will find grace to help us
> when we need it most." Heb 4:16 (NLT)*

The Gospels show us the reality of the many trials that Jesus went through during His life on earth, from the temptation by Satan in the wilderness, to his betrayal by Judas in the Garden of Gethsemane. And yet, "He was without sin" (Hebrews 4:15.)

He stood firm, at great cost, during the hardest moments of His life as God the Son, and today He stands with us and for us during our hardest trials.

This should make us shout for joy!

In Hebrews 4:16, the author calls us to "hold firmly to the faith that we profess" and then calls us to "be bold" as we come before the Throne of Grace.

We are to be bold as we pray for our needs and the needs of others:

"Let us hold fast the confession of our hope without wavering, for He who promised is faithful." Hebrews 10:23.

This boldness is to be reflected in our prayer life and in our testimony to others. We have access to the Holy of Holies through the blood of Christ that redeemed us. Indeed, as we enter our prayer time, we step onto holy ground.

We too often criticize other religions for their legalism concerning their prayer rituals. And yet, many times these devotees are much more faithful than we are, as they come before their gods and plea for their needs. That is a shame!

Sometimes our reluctance in praying for our needs and others' may suggest a lack of gratitude for the amazing access we have into God's presence.

Jesus is always there, eager to be summoned by us.

Let us come into His presence more often! Let us bow before Him with expectant hearts, knowing that He who promised is indeed faithful!!

In His book *Emotions – Confront the Lies, Conquer with Truth,* Pastor and author Dr. Charles Stanley talks about prayer as being the first step of conquering our anxieties:

"I cannot stress this enough: Your personal relationship with the Father is everything — the most important aspect of your life, without exception. It is the basis of your joy, peace, fulfillment, worth and success. Through communion with Him, you can find answers to your questions about who He is and who He created you to be. Being on your knees in close, personal interaction with Him is how you will surely triumph over all your fears. As I always say, your intimacy with God — His first priority for your life — determines the impact of your life. (…)"[4]

What a Joy to know that we have a friend before the Throne of Grace, and that He is the Almighty's Son! What a privilege to be able to commune with the Creator, one-on-one! Not only do we have ample access to the Throne of Grace, but we also have freedom of speech with Him who sits thereon.

We can draw near with confidence!

Overwhelming Love

When I think about my trials, I think of our Savior at the cross, blood flowing down His precious face, as the crowd for whom He would willingly die shouted "crucify Him!"

I'm reminded that my sin shouted "crucify Him" at the foot of that cross.

I remember that He chose to die to become the One who would fill the gap between me and a perfect, Holy God.

Why? For love. Overwhelming, amazing love.

When I think of my trials in light of eternity, of my wants in light of the surpassing riches of knowing my Savior, they pale in contrast.

When I think that my Jesus is seated in the high heaven, at God's right hand and that He is interceding for me, I am filled with the wonder, yet assurance that God hears my prayers. It makes me want to bring all my sorrows, my doubts and all my joys to my Father. It excites me to think that He cares. And that He can do anything.

In the closet, in the park, or at the kitchen sink, He gives me glimpses of His amazing grace, eternal and unfailing love. And yes, He even sends me that wind to lift my wings up when I am too weak to fly.

I pray that you feel challenged to spend time with the Architect of your Faith Bridge, listening to Him obediently, learning to expectantly stretch your wings out by faith, knowing that He wants to help you soar above all challenges you face.

Chapter 7

Breaking ground

"We turn to God for help when our foundations are shaking, only to learn that it is God who is shaking them. Charles C. West

The noise was quite unbearable. Our conversation had to stop when we approached the construction site. After finishing at the High Museum of Art, Dad and I walked up Peachtree Street for a stroll around the city. Large construction crates could be spotted in the area, as new buildings sprung up all over midtown Atlanta.

I stopped beside one particular construction site,from where the intense noise came. Peeking through a hole, I saw a sturdy worker operating a jackhammer. Sweat poured down his face as he used the drill to break through some stubborn old foundation.

The noise was deafening; the effort, seemingly back breaking

The site was filled with people working to ensure that the foundation of this new building would withstand the test of weather and time. Backhoes were digging deep. Hammers, pickaxes and shovels moved up and down rhythmically in the workers' hands.

Before the beautiful building can embellish the Atlanta skyline and invite new tenants in, there has to be major ground breaking.

It's noisy. Dirty. Ugly.

But it has to happen.

Before any construction starts, there must be ground breaking. Whether a building or a bridge, before any structure is driven into the ground, the workers need to sift the soil to remove rocks and clear the path for the foundations to be installed.

So it is with our lives.

We are surrounded by a culture that claims that if we are hurting, we must have done something wrong.

As I mentioned before, that is an unbiblical and biased thought.

As I mentioned on Chapter 2, there is no question that many of the trials we face in life are natural consequences of our poor choices and our sin. It's the natural law of cause and effect.

However, as I have also mentioned before, if you are a child of God and you're walking in obedience to His voice, the trials you face may actually be tools used by our loving Father to either eliminate what does not belong in your life, or strengthen your testimony and prepare you to fulfill His calling for your life.

My objective in this chapter is to encourage you to understand that God often brings us to our knees, before he starts building a solid foundation upon our lives. Strongholds are like rocks in the soil of our hearts. They need to be removed so that the stakes of our Twelve-Inch Faith Bridge are successfully driven into the ground. The alabaster box had to be broken above Jesus' feet so that the precious oil could anoint the Master and fill the room with its sweet aroma. Likewise, only God knows exactly what He has planned to accomplish in us and through us. He knows how He wants us to serve Him. And many times our trials are used to expose our weaknesses, strengthen our abilities and even help develop our spiritual gifts.

The very first lesson in the process is this — we must trust his methods.

When we turn our attention from our pain to God's plan, we gain a fresh perspective into each valley and we also learn what true gratitude is about: focusing on the Giver, not His gifts.

That's a huge lesson in itself.

In this chapter, I'd like to bare my soul as I share stories of difficult trials I've encountered and how they were used by God to make me aware of strongholds that needed to be surrendered, strengthen my faith and give me a testimony of victory and unshaken faith through difficult circumstances.

Breaking ground through Illness

"You watched me as I was being formed in utter seclusion, as I was woven together in the dark of the womb. You saw me before I was born. Every day of my life was recorded in your book. Every moment was laid out before a single day had passed. Psalm 139:15-16 (NLT)

On October 2010 I was invited to become the Prayer Director of our church's choir. For over a year, I had the privilege to lead an amazing group of prayer warriors as we interceded for the needs of our choir family.

Our group constantly cried out to God on behalf of our brothers and sisters who went through terrible hardships, from divorce to tragic death, and terminal illnesses.

I would often share these prayer requests with my husband and we would pray together. Invariably, at the end of our conversation, we would remind each other of a saying that we heard years ago: *"A phone call can change everything you know about life in an instant. And everyone will get that phone call one day."*

On February 8, 2012 I received that "phone call" in the form of a doctor's visit. I had been experiencing abdominal pain for a couple of days and the pain became almost unbearable that morning. Because of previous health history, my doctor rushed me to the ER for a CT scan of my abdomen. The exam revealed a ruptured ovarian cyst, the culprit of the excruciating pain.

In the meantime, however, to our surprise, the doctors found a mass in my kidney. Two days later, I sat at the urologist office as I was told I had kidney cancer.

My "phone" had rung.

Proving that His Grace is indeed sufficient

"But he said to me, "My grace is sufficient for you, for my power is made perfect in weakness." Therefore I will boast all the more gladly about my weaknesses, so that Christ's power may rest on me."
2 Corinthians 12:9 (NIV)

As I heard the doctor tell me the news, various thoughts raced through my mind:

"I am not supposed to have cancer. I don't have any history in my family. I'm fairly young. I eat healthy. What on earth?"

And then the doctor uttered these words, these amazing words that changed the way I looked at that valley in an instant: "this ovarian cyst may have saved your life. This cancer is a silent killer and most people don't have any symptoms until the cancer is advanced and metastasized. This is really good news."

Pause. First tears ran down my face. Pause. Blessed ovarian cyst. Pause. Praise Your Name, Abba Father! Pause. You are with me. All fear is gone.

Pause. Amazing, indescribable, unfathomable grace poured down on my life.

I don't claim to understand all facets of God's grace, but I certainly experienced it in a whole new dimension during those days. My Bible stayed open to Psalm 139 for many weeks, and as I read this wonderful passage, I started to visualize different ways in which God has taken care of me throughout my life.

I could see the Great Master, shaping my innermost being as I was but a seed in my mother's womb.

I could see the Merciful Father, patiently waiting for me to turn to Him as, like the prodigal son, I pursued everything but Him for far too many years.

I saw Him mercifully nudging me to surrender it all to Him, even as a Christian, as I many times leaned to my own understanding instead of trusting Him blindly.

And finally, I saw Romans 8:28 in lively colors before me, as something that caused me great pain was used to potentially save my life.

"And we know that God causes all things to work together for good to those who love God, to those who are called according to His purpose." (NASB)

And we know

Oh, my friends, what a deep, marvelous truth that Paul, inspired by the Holy Spirit of God delivers in the beginning of this most loved verse of Scripture: we KNOW.

We may not *feel like* God works all things together for our good, but we KNOW.

This truth must be in the forefront of every trial we face. Because, honestly, when you are told you have cancer, or your spouse tells you that he or she does not love you anymore, or your child has walked away from God and is living in bondage and rebellion against everything you taught him or her, how on earth, my friend, how can we *feel* like these things are working together for our good? We can't!

Our minds will want to despair and our hearts will tend to give up and rebel. We will feel like quitting.

It is then that you must admonish your soul, as the psalmist does on Psalm 42:5:

"Why am I discouraged? Why is my heart so sad? I will put my hope in God! I will praise him again— my Savior and my God!" (NLT)

Consider it all joy is not a based on your feelings — It's a choice!

"Consider it all joy, my brethren, when you encounter various trials, knowing that the testing of your faith produces endurance.
And let endurance have its perfect result, so that you may be perfect and complete, lacking in nothing." James 1:2-5

As I sought God after I was told I had kidney cancer, I remembered that only two months before the diagnosis I had spent a long time praying and asking God to show me what He wanted me to prioritize for 2012.

The list was pretty easy:

1. Knowing Him more;
2. Enjoying my family more;
3. Serving Him through my ministry.

While praying for that year, I remember distinctly telling Him to do whatever He wished with my life in order to bring Him glory and so that I'd know Him more intimately.

Two days before the diagnosis, I came across James 1:2-5 and felt compelled to write it down in a 3x5 card and post it on my kitchen sink window. The night I came home after the doctor's visit there were two things that God kept reminding me:

Number One: the fact that I had asked him to do whatever He pleased with my life in order to bring Him glory.

Number Two: He had told me, two days before, to count it all joy.

This verse could easily be misunderstood, had Paul not followed his explanation on what the "ALL" meant:

We are to count our tribulations and our trials as joy.

What a strange, utterly crazy thought for those who don't understand the love of a Father who wishes to bring His children into a deep knowledge of Him.

Paul is saying that our trials produce in us an endurance and faith that otherwise can never be accomplished. Think about it: how can we see His miraculous healing, if we don't go through pain? How can we feel His all comforting presence, if we are never alone? How can we experience the joy of deliverance if we were never in bondage?

Bitter . . . or better?

At the end of every shocking encounter with painful situations in life, we are left with two simple choices: we can choose to become bitter, or we can choose to become better.

In the first process, you will allow the world, the doctors, your mind, the devil, and even your well intentioned friends to determine how you will respond.

Actually, this road is pretty easy to navigate. All you need to do is to feel sorry for yourself, allowing fear and doubt to permeate your mind and do nothing about it.

You can choose to numb yourself with the help of pain killers, alcohol, drugs, sex or any other activity that will get your mind off of your problems.

You will find momentary pleasure and you may even forget your pain for a short time. But at the end of this road, you will find yourself bitter, empty and lost.

The second road is God's path for His children.

Your first response will probably be like everyone else's reaction to traumatic news. You'll cry, you'll hurt and you may even despair.

But then you must choose to stop and look up.

You should then remind yourself that your loving God, who hand-crafted you in your mother's wombs, whose thoughts about you are to prosper you, never to harm you (Jeremiah 29:11), who promised never to leave you nor forsake you (Joshua 1:5), has allowed this trial for a reason.

Then you must *choose* to start worshiping Him before you even understand where you are going and certainly even if you don't "feel" like it, simply because you're determined that you KNOW that He is working it all for your good.

You choose to believe Him at His Word, instead of allowing your mind to wander to places of hopelessness and depression.

You choose to wait expectantly upon His deliverance. You choose to trust that, even if He does not remove your trial, even if your outcome is a far cry from your version of a happy ending, He is still in control and He will reward your faith and faithfulness in this life and in the life to come.

You tell your fearful heart what to believe.

This road leads to life everlasting.

This road leads to an intimate, precious relationship with the Father that can potentially change your life and impact the world around you.

This road will make you better.

When I was told I had cancer, I didn't know the end of my story. I became so overwhelmed by the fact that God had graciously revealed the cancer in such an early stage.

Don't get me wrong. I had my moments. That was my third

major surgery in less than six years. So there were days when I felt depressed and fearful.

But I made a deliberate choice. I chose to praise Him because, although I would lose part of an organ, that loss should mean that I would gain many more years to raise my girls. I chose to believe God at His Word and claim the truth of Romans 8:28 to my life. I chose to tell my heart the truth about my God.

Thus the breaking ground process accomplished what God had planned.

Breaking ground through loneliness

It was Friday night. I absently stared at the television, thinking about how lonely I felt. Looking through my phone book, I knew that the options were not good. The friends who would be available on a Friday night would quickly offer me a tour back into my life before Christ ... Places I knew not to visit anymore.

My new Christian friends were all busy with their husbands and family.

It was me, my TV ... and ... my Bible.

I glanced down and picked it up. A new Christian, I had heard that Jesus was all I needed, but was unsure of how to let Him fill the void. My weekends had been busy for as long as I remembered, filled with friends and many invitations. However, several months earlier, I had attended a retreat that forever changed my life. I surrendered my life to Christ that beautiful September morning and experienced an unprecedented joy and peace.

I spent the following weeks and months on a spiritual high, attending a new Christian discipleship class, prayer meetings and various church functions. I had made several new friends, but they were, well ... new. And most of them were married, anyway.

Loneliness filled my heart on the weekends.

That particular weekend was the hardest of all.

As I held my Bible, tears streamed down my face.

One of my best friends of eight years had turned her back on me. We attended college together. I was the friend who would not leave when her dad tragically died. I left my family at Christmas for the first time in 23 years and jumped on a 12-hour bus trip to be beside her that first Christmas after her dad's accident. I invited her to live with me when she decided to come back to town. We had a great time together for a year. But as I made the choice to follow Christ, she ended our friendship in a very hurtful way.

That was the last drop in the bucket.

"Jesus, I thought you would fill my life, not empty it!" I cried out.

It was there, lying on my couch, that I heard Him whisper in my heart for the first time.

"I am preparing the soil for new sowing, for a new harvest."

It was then that I saw it. I had a vision.

As in a dream, I saw a large, bare field. The soil showed places where trees once stood. It looked desolate. Ugly, even. Then I saw seeds coming down from the heavens, falling inside each hole on the ground. And finally, I saw the same field, green and full of beautiful, lush, tall trees.

"Behold, I am making all things new," I heard.

"The Lord said to Gideon, "I will deliver you with the 300 men who lapped and will give the Midianites into your hands; so let all the other people go, each man to his home." Judges 7:7

Twenty years have passed since that day…

…and I behold the harvest. I see God's vision fulfilled. I can close my eyes and see the faces. My husband, our two daughters and wonderful, truthful friends throughout the years, planted in the field of my life. Besides one very best friend from my youth and my immediate family, they are all new.

They have all been planted by Yahweh's faithful hands.

And they have flourished and yielded fruits of joy, peace, and patience.

True friendship. True love.

I stand amazed.

The vision was hard to believe at the time when loneliness filled my days. When God removed what I thought was true love ... and those whom I considered real friends. He plucked them all, one by one, and left me wondering whether I'd ever feel loved again.

But before He planted a new harvest in my life, He had to teach me to make Jesus my all in all. He wanted me to invite Jesus to become my very best friend.

Instead of giving in to the feelings of loneliness and depression, I sought His face. I made the Bible my greatest companion. I woke up in the middle of the night to talk to my Savior and I started serving Him at church.

And before I realized it, He started planting beautiful new seeds into my life.

God showed me that, just as He gave Gideon victory over mighty enemies with a small army of faithful servants, His children don't need 10,000 soldiers to win life's battles. When God is in control, He weeds out the unfaithful, and fills in the void in our lives with the 300 faithful few.

IN. HIS. TIME.

Gideon was afraid of not having enough. He couldn't see how he would defeat his powerful enemy with such a small army.

You may not see how your life can continue without a particular person. Or how you can give up your old friends and still have joy.

I challenge you to trust Him.

Trust that He is weeding out the unfaithful, cleaning out the soil, preparing it to yield a new harvest.

All He needs is your heart and your surrendered trust.

I promise that one day you'll stand amazed, as you contemplate the lush green fields that Yahweh will plant on your current barren land.

And as you give yourself to Him, believe me: He will give all back to you.

Pressed down, shaken together and running over. (Luke 6:38)

Because that is the kind of friend He is.

Just trust His pruning. Trust His plucking.

He only cuts out what doesn't belong, anyway.

Breaking ground through financial loss

As I glanced up from reading my magazine, my husband's somber expression made me freeze.

"I need to talk to you."

"Ok." I closed the magazine.

"We have thirteen dollars in the bank."

"Come again?" I said.

"Thirteen dollars. And the mortgage is due in two weeks."

I felt a little dizzy. I knew our finances were not good, but I didn't think they were that bad.

My husband had lost his job four months before and we had exhausted our savings. We had a seven-month old baby and I was at home with her. In the aftermath of September 11th 2001, no one was hiring.

We were scared.

But instead of despairing, we chose to pray.

As we knelt on the living room floor, we cried out to the Owner of the universe. We affirmed our trust in His Word. We were bringing our tithe into His house. Even a tithe from our unemployment earnings. Therefore, we claimed His promise of Malachi 4: *He would provide.*

That very day we received a phone call.

A recruiter had a temporary assignment as a consultant for my husband. He would make more an hour than he'd ever made as an employee.

He was out of a full time job for eighteen months.

We never missed our mortgage.

What did we do?

We believed.

This was only one of the financial trials we faced. Several years after that we lost a good deal of money on a business venture. It was many years before we were able to eradicate that debt.

During those years, we did not have everything we wanted, but God provided what we needed. Even if He did it in the eleventh hour.

He has never forsaken us.

Your experience may be different. You may be in much bigger financial need than I've ever experienced. But realize this: His promises are the same for each one of His children.

What I do realize, however, is that each lesson is different.

I had to learn trust. I had to learn to be more responsible with my finances. I had to learn to have a budget. I had to learn to be content with little.

Your experience in the valley of financial burdens may be different.

But there's a lesson nonetheless.

The breaking ground of financial needs has the potential to break marriages ... or make them stronger than ever.

The breaking ground of financial needs has the potential to make you a more giving person ... or stingier than ever.

Once again ... the choice is yours. But there is no doubt: There is a lesson to be learned, if only to trust Him blindly. You must surrender to the ground breaking lesson He's allowing in your life.

In the meantime, keep telling this unwavering truth about God, your Provider — you may not have everything you want, but He will provide for all your needs.

Breaking ground through mourning

My children and I were singing and dancing around the family room, as the Sister Sledge's 70's hit "We are Family" blared through the stereo speakers. While we giggled together doing silly moves, I realized how long it had been since I had a good belly laugh. The sound of it was even strange to my ears. I realized how sad our home has been since we lost my husband's brother in a tragic accident the year before. I realized how little we had laughed since then.

It was then that God reminded me of the passage in Ecclesiastes where Solomon talked about the different valleys and mountaintops which all people go through.

"There is an appointed time for everything. And there is a time for every event under heaven— A time to give birth and a time to die; A time to plant and a time to uproot what is planted. A time to kill and a time to heal; A time to tear down and a time to build up. A time to weep and a time to laugh; A time to mourn and a time to dance."
Ecclesiastes 3:1-4

I was reminded that these good and bad times are a natural part of the realm in which we live, one of a fallen world. As Solomon wrote these words, the Lord inspired him to compare different circumstances in life to the seasons and natural course of nature.

Just as the night falls, we can be sure that the sun will rise again. Just as the rain comes down, we know that the sun will eventually break through the clouds.

And just as the seasons come and go, faithfully each year, so do the good and bad times in life.

If nature could sing one song, or repeat only one sentence to us through life's valleys, it would be "This too shall pass."

Except death

I have gone through some pretty dark valleys in life. Physical separation from loved ones? Check. Big financial burden? Check. Betrayal of friends? Check. Health problems? Check, check, check!

During all these trials, however, even throughout the hardest of days, my heart has been able to sing a song of praise. But the death of a close relative was not only a new experience to me, it was, by far, the hardest one I've encountered so far.

The truth is, in the physical realm of what we know, we can go through different things with a hope that life will be reinstated to what it once was. You lose a job, there is the almost certainty that you will eventually find work again. You go through a health problem, there is always the hope that God will come forth with a miraculous healing or that the treatment will do its job.

But in the physical realm of what we know, the understanding that you will never hug that person again or talk to them; the separation, even though we know (by faith) that it's just for a while, is very, very hard.

God does not expect it to be different. He knows the pain of losing a loved one. Jesus wept when He heard that his dear friend Lazarus had died (John 11:34-36.) He knew He would see him again soon when he'd call him forth from the dead, but the understanding that death had taken over Lazarus' body was overwhelming to the Master.

David was also overcome with sadness when he heard that his best friend Jonathan had died (2 Samuel 1:26.) This giant of faith, who has written many of the Psalms which fill our hearts with hope and strength through life's hardest valleys, was terribly hurt with his friend's passing.

"O death, where is your victory? O death, where is your sting?"
1 Corinthians 15:55

For those of us who have lost loved ones in the Lord, these verses give us much hope. Paul was talking to the Corinthians about the power over eternal death that Jesus' resurrection has given to His saints.

For those who died in Christ, death has no victory, no sting. For my brother-in-law Donnie, all tears have been wiped away (Revelations 21:4,) there will be no more sickness, no more dying, no more sorrow. He is now reaping his rewards before the Master and enjoying the company of the saints and of the Triune God forever.

For those of us who stay, however, death stings and it hurts a lot. And to say that does not make me a weak Christian.

It makes me a human one.

I know we will all find new joys and sing new songs; we will still laugh and continue to enjoy the days God allows us to live.

But sometimes life just hurts. And it's all right to say that.

It's supposed to. That truth is in the heart of Solomon's discourse on Chapter 3 of Ecclesiastes. Matthew Henry puts it beautifully in his commentary:

> *"There is a time when God's providence calls to weep and mourn, and when man's wisdom and grace will comply with the call, and will weep and mourn, as in times of common calamity and danger, and there it is very absurd to laugh, and dance, and make merry (Isaiah 22:12, 13; Ezekiel 21:10); but then, on the other hand, there is a time when God calls to cheerfulness, a time to laugh and dance, and then he expects we should serve him with joyfulness and gladness of heart."[1]*

Trusting His Sovereignty

There is one unyielding truth that lies in the heart of both the changes in the natural realm, and in the spiritual one. Both nature and men, the weather and our trials, are subject to the sovereignty of Almighty God.

From the most natural things that happen on earth, including raindrops and lightning strikes, to the most life-changing experiences that a child of God can have, including betrayal, cancer and death; all these things are subject to the foreknowledge of God.

Although this has certainly been something that I have affirmed for many years since becoming a Christian, this truth became an important anchor which I clung to when we faced Donnie's tragic death.

We are taught to recite that God is in control, but when life's happenings don't make sense, we must realize that, indeed, He really is in charge.

And we must understand it deep in our souls, not just on the surface.

If you or someone you know is having a hard time because they have lost a loved one, even though you embrace, by faith, that your separation is momentary (life is but a vapor — James 4:14,) that does not change the fact that you are in great pain.

One day, God will restore in your heart the joy that is momentarily gone. And you shall dance again. You shall find new joy; not because you won't miss your loved one any longer, but because we serve a faithful and joyful God. And although there will always be a hole in your heart, a place once filled by someone who is gone from this life forever, your faith in our sovereign God will bring a new song to your heart.

The faith that assures you that your separation is but for a moment will bring you through.

But even the type of faith that survives the valley of the shadow of death is a choice.

As quoted from the devotional "Streams in the Desert" for September 26:

"As believers, We live by Faith and not by sight (2 Corinthians 5:7)- God never wants us to live by our feelings. Our inner self may want us to live by feelings, and Satan may want us to, but God wants to face the facts, not feelings. He wants us to face the facts of Christ and His finished and perfect works for us. And once we face and believe these precious facts, and believe them simply because God says they are facts, He will take care of our feelings."[2]

Do you realize the power behind these words? Any feelings we face — from the fear of failing health, to the excruciating pain of losing a loved one, can be overcome when we face the facts of God's character and unfailing love!

Thanking Him for the ground breaking process

It is hard to focus on the goodness of God when dark clouds settle over our lives. It's not easy to stay focused on Him when our health is failing … or death reaches our family … or our finances are collapsing. And yet, I am typing these words with the certainty of a person who has been through many such trials. Some of which I still face.

What I have learned from the lesson in each valley is not that the experience is necessarily brief; rather, the length of duration does not matter — what matters is that we should not forget that our Shepherd is with us!

"Even though I walk through the valley of the shadow of death,
I fear no evil, for You are with me; Your rod and Your staff,
they comfort me." Psalm 23:4

Oh, that we would grasp with all our heart and soul the power behind this truth: that the lesson in the shadow of the valley of death is not a message of despair, but rather, thanks!

"Surely goodness and loving kindness will follow me all the days of my
life, and I will dwell in the house of the Lord forever." Psalm 23:6

Indeed, in this verse of this most beloved Psalm, David is shouting out to you and me:

Is it dark? I know you can't see it, but the Shepherd is holding your hand. You shall not stumble and fall. Thank Him for His protection in the valley.

Are you tired and weary? He is ready to lead you beside the still waters and the green pastures that you will find in His presence

(Psalm 23:2). Open your Bible to Psalms. Meditate upon His faithfulness, goodness and eternal mercy. Thank Him for His rest in the valley.

Remember this: A valley must be surrounded by mountains and each mountain has its apex. Your journey will take you there. As a matter of fact, you may just be on the mountainside and you don't realize it. Indeed, the journey gets harder, steeper, rougher, as you get ready to conquer that mountain. As you climb, God is teaching you diligence and trust. He is strengthening the muscles of your faith.

The mountaintop is a promise. The valley is a holy teaching ground.

As we walk through the valleys of death, loneliness, pain or financial distress, let us trust the Master with each lesson He has for us. And let us hold on to Him as He walks beside us all the way to the mountaintop.

That is what true, unshakable thanksgiving is all about.

Trust the process

We don't see the complete picture of our future. Only God knows the plans he has for us. He knows the things that we need to learn, areas where we need to mature, or weaknesses that will prevent us from reaching our full potential.

And I fully believe that many of our trials are nothing but the breaking in of that stubborn ground where we insist on planting our feet.

A beautiful and new building cannot be erected on an old, crumbling foundation. There needs to be shaking and breaking.

We may need to surrender some things.

It may be habits that need to be overcome.

Or fears that need to be conquered.

It may be bitterness that needs to be defeated or people who need to be removed from our lives.

It's painful. Noisy.

And yet, so very necessary.

Of course there are tragedies that happen in our world that don't make sense. But as a follower of Christ, we must choose to believe that God is not finished making us. And yes, the process is often painful. But as I look back at whom I once was and whom I am today, I can see the progress.

Undoubtedly, were it not for different painful situations I have encountered, I would not be the same person. It does not make it any easier, but I have decided not to question the Architect. I trust Him because He knows what I need in order to become what He has called me to be.

And I certainly know that there are some old, crumbling structures that need to be removed.

What about you?

Chapter 8

One step at a time

"How poor are they that have not patience! What wound did ever heal but by degrees?" William Shakespeare

"I'm going to Michael Bublé's concert tomorrow night."

By the look on my face, my friend knew that I had no idea of whom she was talking about. Later on, I decided that I must be living in a different planet: I was probably the only girl who had never heard of the famous Canadian singer.

When I got home later that evening, I decided to do some research and find out exactly how Michael became a world sensation overnight. So, I Googled his name. In an instant, Wikipedia provided detailed information about his life. Before starting to learn about him, I was almost aggravated by the fact that this guy came out of nowhere and seemed to have become an instant success.

Until I found out that there is absolutely nothing instant about his career!

Bublé worked hard and waited for a break for many years. He was not an overnight success. He had to wait for almost 20 years before his name became a pop music sensation. And although I don't know the guy, a quick look at his life made me realize that he is another classic case of an irresistibly powerful combination for success: patience and perseverance. These two traits are becoming very rare these days.

We look at famous people around us and almost resent their apparent quick path to fame. But the truth of the matter is that not many truly talented artists, writers or people of prominence get to the top without much hard work, failure, perseverance and patience.

We live in a "Bibbi-de-bob-adee-boo" society. We all wish to become Cinderellas at the wave of a magic wand. We want to finish college and become the CEO of the company in a year. We decide to start a blog today and hope to have 1 million followers in a month. We wish to lose 30 pounds in two weeks. Bibbi-de-bob-adee-boo!

That's why so many of us become discouraged with God.

In our pursuit of having strong faith — that type of faith that navigates life's rough waters with confidence, we can't expect to reach our destination without hard work, perseverance and patience. Sorry, but Our Faith Bridge cannot be built at the wave of a magic wand.

My purpose in this chapter is to remind you that God's ultimate desire for us is to change us, transform us into the likeness of His Son, Jesus Christ. Therefore, the process of building our Twelve-Inch Faith Bridge takes time, diligence and patience.

God is not partial to instant gratification. Unlike us, he knows exactly when we are ready to receive our promises and dreams. The waiting process is designed to be a growth process.

There are flaws in our character that will only be remedied if we are exposed to trials, failures and much perseverance. If God gives us a vision or promise, we must grab the fact that we cannot become great at whatever we are called to do unless we allow circumstances to develop our character, chipping away imperfections and preparing us for success. That's why building strong faith requires diligence and willingness to change.

And we do that one step at a time.

One step towards obedience

When my daughters were toddlers, I remember becoming very impatient with their tendency to disobey me over and over again. When I confronted them, they would always apologize for the disobedience and promise they'd "never do it again."

Of course that only lasted a couple of days.

I remember getting very frustrated by their disobedience on the same little things. I cringed at the fact that I had to repeat myself one hundred times to my little children regarding what they should and shouldn't do. I'd get upset that they just didn't seem to get it.

Then God, in His amazing long-suffering and grace, would invariably hold up a mirror to my face: "Hello! Are you any different?"

The story of the people of Israel is like our story. He delivered them out of bondage through an amazing sequence of miracles: the plagues in Egypt, parting the Red Sea, providing the *manna* in the desert, victorious wars against much more powerful enemies, the surprising and miraculous fall of the walls of Jericho.

Yet, they continuously doubted, compromised and disobeyed.

"Now the angel of the LORD came up from Gilgal to Bochim And he said, " I brought you up out of Egypt and led you into the land which I have sworn to your fathers; and I said, 'I will never break My covenant with you, and as for you, you shall make no covenant with the inhabitants of this land; you shall tear down their altars. But you have not obeyed Me; what is this you have done?" Judges 2:1-3

For forty years, it was one step forward … and two steps backward.

Doesn't it sound familiar? I can certainly relate. I've seen God's deliverance. He has been Jehovah Jireh, my provider, Jehovah Rafa, my healer and my strong tower in times of trouble.

And yet, in the past, when facing trials, I had a hard time acting on the belief that He would show up again.

Indeed, our natural tendency is to take matters into our own hands, thus not realizing that we are indeed building altars to the gods of self-indulgence: our timing, our things, and our plans. I can't help but imagine God saying (just as He said to Israel) "What is this you have done?"

The awesome covenant that God made with His people requires only two things from us: to love and obey Him. All our good works and church activities together cannot make up for not fulfilling our part in the Covenant He made with us:

"Has the LORD as much delight in burnt offerings and sacrifices as in obeying the voice of the LORD? Behold, to obey is better than sacrifice, and to heed than the fat of rams." 1 Samuel 15:22

And yet, we tarry obedience … or neglect it altogether.

One step into building a strong Faith Bridge is to obey the Father promptly, lest we slow down the process.

Delayed obedience equals disobedience

When God gives us an instruction, we are never to second-guess Him. When He says, "Give this up!" we are not to rationalize His instructions. As children, we should say, "Yes, Lord."

That's what I so hope my children will learn to do by watching my walk: simply obey. No excuses or questioning. Period.

"Trust in the Lord with all your heart, lean not to your own understanding, in all your ways acknowledge Him, and He will direct your paths". Proverbs 3:5-6

There is a place in our walk with the Lord where the rubber meets the road. It's the place where our worship songs are not just a feel good moment; rather, they become our hearts' song.

The place where the rubber meets the road is where my faith surpasses my reasoning. It's where my obedience does not always make sense and it will not always be popular. It's where my obedience may mean I lose possessions, position and friends.

The place where the rubber meets the road is where when God says "Do it," I get up and start moving. It's the place where when He says: "Be still," I sit back down and remind myself that He is God. (Psalm 46:10).

The place where the rubber meets the road is where my faith is tested and where my rough edges are sanded. It's the place that I get on my knees more often. It's where I feel His presence more real than ever. It's where I grow the most and it's where I get closer to Him.

It's the exact place where God wants me to be.

What trials are you are currently facing? Are you so busy trying to get out of the tedious place of your trial, that you will miss the blessings God has for you if you withstand the tribulation with Him, one step at a time?

Do you realize that God may just be waiting for you to be still, to worship and trust Him in spite of your circumstances?

Obey Him and watch Him work.

Obedience is one step in the right direction!

One step towards courage

I was lying on a stretcher at the ER while a doctor and two nurses surrounded me. The doctor's hand rested on my arm: "You're not dying, Patricia. There's nothing wrong with you. We've checked it all." And yet, no matter how many times he repeated that medical truth, my brain told me something different.

I was dying. I just knew I was.

A panic attack. Another one.

My personal hell on earth.

Fear is noise that keeps you from hearing God's voice

Never have I experienced this truth in a more powerful way than during the year I became a Christian.

It happened twenty years ago, but I can vividly recall how fear paralyzed my thinking and my life. Extreme stress took me over the edge and the devil milked it for all it was worth.

He breathed defeat and death into my ears … and I believed it.

Fear is real. It's real for the strongest believers, as much as it is for the youngest in the faith. The difference is that, as we grow in knowledge of God and as we experience His sovereignty and power, we become more equipped to overcome all fear.

That's where Joshua was in his faith walk as God charged him to take possession of the Promised Land (Joshua 1). Fearful … yet equipped.

"No man will be able to stand before you all the days of your life. Just as I have been with Moses, I will be with you; I will not fail you or forsake you." Joshua 1:5

He had been with Moses as God empowered Israel's leader to accomplish the impossible. Over and over again, he watched as Yahweh took care of His people.

Now the giants waited across the Jordan. They were bigger, mightier than Israel.

Yet, God said, "Do not be afraid. Go. Get. Them."

All he needed was the courage to obey and take the first step.

Scary charge

Joshua knew that he had to lead God's people into battle against a stronger and better prepared enemy. Don't you know he was scared! We can actually catch a glimpse of Joshua's spirit regarding the task ahead of him by the fact that God commanded him to be strong and courageous four times on Chapter One alone.

Joshua was afraid. So am I.

Every time I am confronted with giants that are bigger and stronger than I am, or big challenges that evoke defeat, my heart wavers.

Being afraid is being human.

But if we are to get to our Promised Land, we certainly need courage. We cannot shrink at the sight of a road block ... or a powerful enemy.

As we read through the first chapter of Joshua, we see God challenging us to trust Him as He promises victory. In this passage, the Lord of the battle teaches us what we must do when challenged to do something bigger than what we believe we can handle; or when we face the giants of opposition and trials.

God actually teaches us how to overcome fear and gain supernatural courage to build our faith, step by step:

Step #1: Look at the past to trust God for the task ahead:

"As I was with Moses, so will I be with you" Joshua 1:5a

Can you look back in your life and see the times that God brought you victory against all odds?

The disease that was healed, the prodigal child who returned home, the broken relationship that was mended.

Joshua had been with Moses in the wilderness, and watched as God delivered Israel from Pharaoh's hand and provided *manna* for His people...

He saw God's glory in Moses' face when he descended Mount Sinai with the tablets of the law.

He had experienced God.

Therefore, he drew his strength from his experience and belief that God was going ahead of him into battle. He then took the first step forward.

Indeed, any time in our lives that God calls us to do something bigger than ourselves, looking back is a way of gaining the courage to take one more step with God. The reason for Joshua's victory, was because he remembered, believed, and therefore he obeyed.

He was not victorious because of his talents, or his ability to fight the battles, but because he knew that just as it had been in the wilderness, God would fight the battle for him. Again.

Step #2: Remind yourself that you're not alone.

"I will not fail you, nor forsake you".

Not only did God promise victory, He promised that He would be with Joshua in battle.

And so it is with us as we face life's greatest challenges: He will not fail us when we are weak, nor will He forsake us when we feel inadequate. He gives us the task, and He promises to empower us to accomplish it.

Our acceptance of a charge given by God opens His heart and He fills us with His grace, thus empowering us to fulfill His plan for our lives.

If He tells you to go, there's no question about it. He is set ahead of you, opening doors and preparing the battle grounds. So, you should indeed, GO!

All that is needed is a little courage to take the first step … and then the next.

Step #3: Take a Deep Breath and Jump!

"Be strong and courageous! Do not tremble and be dismayed, for the Lord your God is with you wherever you go." (Joshua 1:9)

We cannot easily count the "fear not's" of the Bible. These are not just soothing words, and they are very often a call to battle and victory. To be a follower of Jesus requires strength of character and courage to stand alone in many circumstances.

In Chapter Eleven of the book of Hebrews, almost each time that the author refers to one of his saints' faith, he attributes their greatness to their courage.

Each giant of faith had to defeat the giants of fear and feelings of inadequacy … They had to courageously take a giant leap of faith before God delivered. Provided. Healed.

Indeed, we can choose to shrink in fear and live a mediocre life. Or choose to say yes to God's charge to conquer the impossible and stand in awe as He delivers His supernatural best.

Step #4: Surrender to His Word

"(…) Be careful to do according to all the law which Moses My servant commanded you; do not turn from it to the right or to the left, so that you may have success wherever you go." (Joshua 1:7)

The world thinks we are crazy when we declare that success follows submission and obedience. By society's viewpoint, obedience is a sign of weakness. The strong control and the weak are controlled — that's the world's order.

For Joshua, on the other hand, success would only come as he was controlled by God.

God told Joshua that, in order to succeed, he must obey ALL God's instructions and His law. Not just partially, not with some personal twist here and there, but the entire law.

God was actually giving Joshua these instructions because He knew there would be times when Joshua would not exactly SEE where God was taking Him, and therefore His law would guide him.

So it is in our lives, as many times we cannot see where God's paths are leading us.

That is when we must read His Word, obey it entirely, and trust that "He who began a good work in us will be faithful to complete it." Philippians 1:6.

Conquering fear follows courage. Courage follows obedience. Obedience follows surrender.

That's Heaven's order.

Fear is indeed the father of every failure

Fear of conflict, fear of shame, fear of rejection, fear that God will leave us alone and our prayers unanswered.

Fear exaggerates the problems, hates the tasks ahead of us, and postpones obedience. Fear is crippling and fear does NOT come from God!

Whatever giant you are facing today, remember Yahweh's encouragement as He repeated it again and again throughout His Word:

"Don't be afraid, for I am with you. Don't be discouraged, for I am your God. I will strengthen you and help you. I will hold you up with my victorious right hand." (Isaiah 41:10)

Is there a "next step" that God wants you to take and that you are fiercely avoiding, out of disobedience or fear?

It could be sharing Jesus with someone you know…

It could be bringing your tithe and offerings into the house of God …

It could be breaking up with the boyfriend or girlfriend whom you know is not God's best for you...

It could be simply taking the first step and saying YES to a calling ... to go on a mission trip ... to teach a Sunday School class ... or minister to someone in need.

Whatever small or big step God tells you to take, even if you feel inadequate to carry it out, obey Him TODAY. Do not wait; do not procrastinate. Forget the excuses. Delayed obedience is disobedience and creates dangerous spiritual static in your life, preventing you from hearing the Father's voice.

Ask Him to give you the courage to take the first step. Say "Yes, Lord. No more excuses."

Next, get up and get moving. You have no time to waste.

Move forward ... One step at a time...

Obey...

Be confident...

And as you move into the giants' territory ... remember:

If God is for you, with you, in you ... who or what on earth can be against you? Romans 8:31

A Word of Caution to the hasty!

Some of us may be too slow to move. However, some of the more eager Jesus followers may just a bit too hasty to take the next step.

I understand that group pretty well. I'm in it. I have no problem jumping in and taking a challenge that God presents. My problem is the other side of the spectrum. You may be able to relate.

Patience is a virtue I don't naturally possess. Only with the help of the Holy Spirit am I able to wait upon God. A natural "type A" personality, it's hard for me to stand on the sidelines, not moving a finger. My tendency is to say "Yes, I'll do it!" and to get busy making things happen instead of waiting on God to show me what to do next.

Much like some of you, I want it and I want it NOW.

This trait can be very valuable, though. Sanguines are usually the world's go-getters. They are boisterous, bubbly, chatty, openly emotional, true social extroverts. They are Ronald Reagan, Bill Clinton, Franklin Roosevelt and Peter the apostle, to name a few. They have changed history and impacted the world with their ideas, boldness and often lack of restraint.

But as many virtues as people with this type of personality possess, their strength can also be their biggest weakness.

Invariably, because of their honest need to accomplish and finish what they start, they have a hard time waiting.

Especially on God.

For the Christian, the problem with that concept is that God's ways are not our ways.

His thoughts? Much higher than ours (Isaiah 55:8).

He does not operate within our natural reality realm. His definition of success certainly does not match the world's view of success and therefore, He (usually) acts at a much slower pace than we do. Admittedly, He seems sometimes painfully slow. That's because He's not in the business of answering to us. Nor is He that genie, whose job is to make our dreams come true. Rather, He has a definite plan for our lives.

Like I mentioned before, we often are not ready to fulfill His plan for our lives unless He first works on our character. And waiting is certainly one of the tools He uses to make us. Reshape us. Redefine us. And undoubtedly strengthen us for the tasks He has for us.

It all sounds good and makes sense, but exactly how am I supposed to know when to move?

I believe the best question for the boisterous in spirit is this: Exactly how am I supposed to know when NOT to move?

"Your word is a lamp to my feet and a light to my path." Psalm 119:105

The weary traveler walked carefully on the dusty road. It was a dark, starless night. He looked around him and was greeted with sounds of creatures he could not see. In one hand, he carried a sack containing a meager meal and some coins that he hoped to spend renting a room in a nearby town. In the other hand, he carried a lamp. The traveler lifted it up, high above his head, in the hopes of illuminating his surroundings. He put his hand down, then, dismayed. The lamp in his hand shed only enough light to illuminate a small section of the pathway ahead of him. Only enough to see where his next step would fall.

This illustration depicts the type of lamp that the psalmist used to describe what we need in order to follow God.

In Old Testament times, travelers would carry a small oil lamp, the dim light only enough to shine into the steps ahead of the traveler. Likewise, the Word of God is the light which not only drives away the darkness of sin and hopelessness; it also directs us on which way to go.

It's not that I don't believe that God still gives His children prophetic visions regarding His master plan for their lives. I certainly believe He does. However, when it comes to obeying His voice and carrying out His plan, more often than not, He only gives just enough instructions for one step at a time.

Whether we take one step, obediently, and then wait for further instructions, or choose to rush into the future, disregarding His voice … is a matter of TRUST.

At the end of the day, the question we all must ask is … do I trust my Maker with my future?

Or do I think unless I act, and act now, I will miss out?

Do I trust enough to hold all my natural instincts and personality back, submitting to His voice before I take the next step?

Or do I leave the small oil lamp behind, rushing into the darkness with the eagerness of the ungodly?

His Word is a lamp … therefore we must obey its principles if we are to live victoriously.

His Word is light … therefore we must hear His Spirit and obey it, unquestionably, waiting for His instructions before moving forward.

And when we feel rushed to make a decision, we must stop. The only correct immediate answer is:

"I'll pray for direction."

The person, the project, the job should wait. It's all right; God will honor your dependence upon Him.

He promises peace to those who earnestly seek Him. And the peace is the answer you need. Just like that lamp, His peace will guide you into the next step. And then, step by step.

If you commit your ways to the Lord … And trust Him … you need not worry. The promise is that Yahweh Himself, the One who spoke the stars into existence, will act on your behalf. (Proverbs 3:5-6, Psalm 37:5; Lamentations 3:25; Psalm 130:5-6)

You must only complete one step of obedience at a time and then stop. Look up, and wait for His Light to shine down into the next step you'll take, telling what to do next.

Or, better yet! He may just do it for you.

But I feel like I'm going nowhere!

"Then he said, "Throw out your net on the right-hand side of the boat, and you'll get some!" So they did, and they couldn't haul in the net because there were so many fish in it." V.6

They had seen the resurrected Savior. Excitement and renewed faith had fueled them for the road ahead of them. Even so, Simon Peter, Thomas and the sons of Zebedee became discouraged again.

They had been fishing all night long. As the hours progressed, they each grew tired and discouraged. They had bills to pay and mouths to feed. Yet, not a single fish was caught in their large net. As the morning dawned, a Stranger called out from ashore: "Fellows, have you caught any fish". Their hearts sank as they admitted their unsuccessful trip. "Cast the net on the other side," He said. As John realized it was the Lord Who had spoken, excitement built up in their hearts, as fish flooded their net.

Have you ever noticed that when Jesus told his discouraged disciples to cast their nets again, it was right at the same old place where they had caught nothing all night long?

The same seems to happen with us when we find ourselves in the same barren place for a long time. We take a step out of obedience and wait ... and yet, nothing seems to encourage us to remain in that same, empty place.

It could be a disease that lingers ... or a deteriorating relationship.

It could be long-term unemployment ... or an emotional wound that won't heal.

We pray and wait and pray and wait and nothing seems to be moving.

If we could just get off to a brand new place when we get discouraged, casting our nets again would be an easier thing to do! If we could be a different person, or go somewhere new, or do something else it might not be so hard to have fresh faith and new encouragement.

But it is the same old net that caught nothing all night long ... in the same empty sea!

Old temptations call to be overcome. Old relationships call to be healed. Old trials and valleys which we faced yesterday and the day before, call to be faced today. O.n.c.e. A.g.a.i.n.

When Jesus found the disciples failing in their night long fishing trip, He could have told them to take up their nets and follow Him to a new, bountiful area of the sea.

But He didn't. Instead, He told them to win success exactly where they were.

They could have argued with Him. After all, these were professional fishermen! They knew the sea like no one else: "Jesus, you don't understand — we know what we are doing here," they may have been tempted to say.

Instead, they moved their nets, only seven feet across the width of the boat, and cast it on the other side. And as their weary hands obeyed the Master, the bounty came forth.

Do you feel discouraged as each step of obedience seems to be leading you nowhere?

Is it the same boat, the same spot, the same fishing technique, over and over again for months, perhaps years?

Remember: If you are in the center of God's will, walking in obedience with Him, you are where God wants you to be. The circumstances you are in may be uncomfortable, and you may be ready to move on to a better fishing spot. However, unless the Master calls you to move from where you are … Remain …

He is working an eternal fruit eternal in your life. He is molding you as you cast your net over and over again. He is strengthening you as you choose to trust Him, even though you are tired and weary.

In the process of waiting for His deliverance and His provision to come, keep on searching for the Stranger on the shore. Allow His gentle hands to sand the rough edges of your attitude. Keep reading the Instruction Manual He has provided. Keep calling out to Him for deliverance and peace. And by all means, don't be shy! Tell Him exactly how you feel in this barren, lonely place.

He is listening.

And when you feel too tired to go on, remember this: It is the Master Himself, who, after your toilsome, disheartening failures, keeps calling out to you:

"Try again!"

One step at a time. Rome was not built in a day, as the famous maxim states. Neither will your Faith Bridge evolve overnight.

We must remind ourselves that without trials, patience and perseverance, success is unmerited. Cinderellas lose their shoes at midnight and return home in rags and barefoot. And as anxious as I sometimes get to reach my goals and see my dreams come true, I know one day I'll be rewarded for learning my lessons along the way in order to build a solid castle, one stone at a time.

God is still working. Whatever you do, don't ever give up. Remember those who, with faith, perseverance and patience, received their dreams. Many are the witnesses who are living proofs that God helps those who patiently wait and work diligently to reach their goals.

One step at a time.

Chapter 9

The Power of His Word

"We all have our convictions formed by different things, and mine
are informed by my faith, they're informed by the Word of God, and
I found that to be an anchor for me, a compass and a guide for me."
Kirk Cameron – actor, television host, evangelist.

The GPS kept changing our arrival time. When we missed the
turn, the GPS adjusted its direction and we found ourselves arriving
at the destination about ten minutes later than expected. My husband
wasn't all too happy with the new GPS system. The area was unfamiliar.
Unfriendly faces stared at us. We were definitely in the wrong part of
town. But I was not scared. I knew we would be out of the area soon.

My hope was set on the fact that the GPS knew where we
needed to go. It would take a little longer than we thought, but we
would get there. We weren't lost.

I'm certainly grateful for modern GPS systems. When I moved
to America, I remember how hard it was to adapt to the new road
system. I remember the tension building up inside me any time I
was alone and trying to get somewhere new.

And then the wonder of GPS systems happened. I wasn't scared
anymore. I had a guide with me, knowing exactly where I wanted
to go; telling me each time I made the wrong turn and correcting
my wrong, keeping me on course.

GPS systems and the Bible have indeed a lot in common.

A GPS system is an interactive map, which surveys the area and lets us know exactly where to turn in order to get to a certain destination.

If God is the Architect of our Faith Bridge, the Bible is His blueprint. His map.

We must consult it if we are to build a strong Faith Bridge. Ignoring this road map is the same as ignoring the Architect. Because He has poured His soul, His direction, His wisdom and knowledge into crafting the road map that we are to study.

This map is a translation of God's love, wisdom and grace in print. It has answers to all life's questions. It guides us when we are lost and comforts us when we feel like life is taking us nowhere. It points us to the right direction, no matter how many wrong turns we take.

We must study it, know it and cherish it.

But not only is the Bible a road map for living, it's also a mighty weapon to defeat strong enemies and strongholds that have the potential to crack our Faith Bridge.

A defense weapon — the machaira

"And take the helmet of salvation, and the sword of the Spirit, which is the word of God." Ephesians 6:17

The enemy saw it from a distance and shuddered at its sight.

Roman soldiers had a choice of about five different weapons of war. Mostly, the weapons were swords. Among the ones they could use in battle, the *machaira* was certainly the deadliest. Inherited from the Greek army, it could be as long as nineteen inches, but it was often shorter, resembling a dagger; therefore it was usually used in close combat. It was razor sharp on both sides of the blade and its very end turned upward, causing the point of the blade to be extremely sharp and deadly.

After stabbing his enemy and before removing the blade, the soldier would grab the sword tightly and twist it, pulling the man's entrails out as the sword was removed.

Not a pretty sight.

Fierce. Unforgiving. Deadly. That was the *machaira* for its enemies.

And that is the type of sword Paul envisioned when he referred to God's Word while describing the Armor of God in Ephesians 6. The Greek word *machaira,* describing this powerful sword is mentioned several times in the New Testament, always referring to God's Word and the judgment that it brings to the enemy (Eph. 6:17; Heb. 4:12; Rev. 1:16; 2:12), as well as an instrument of God's wrath (Rev. 2:16; 19:15).

I decided I'd check around my house to find out how many *machairas* we own. I counted nine printed versions of the Bible. We also have a Bible study software including all current translations of God's Word, numerous commentaries and dictionaries (loaded on three computers and one tablet), as well as the You Version software, which is loaded on my smart phone and our daughters' iPods.

From what I understand and according to the apostle Paul, the Holbrooks are extremely armed and dangerous!

But … do we realize it?

On Ephesians 6:10, the Holy Spirit reminds us of our true enemy. It is not our health, Ebola, ISIS, the economy, Iran, Russia, North Korea or corrupt politicians. As dark as these forces may be, they are nothing but instruments used by a much higher force, Satan and his army.

"For our struggle is not against flesh and blood, but against the rulers, against the powers, against the world forces of darkness, against the spiritual forces of wickedness in the heavenly places." Ephesians 6:12

I'm afraid we tend to forget that.

If you are a born-again, spirit-filled, heaven-bound Christian, you are at war. And although our ultimate victory has been won by Christ on the cross, we are engaged in battles for our heart, mind and soul every single day. The devil's days are counted and it seems that as time passes, Christians have been increasingly attacked by this Prince of Darkness. And while it has always happened, it seems to me that it has increased in the last while. Satan is undermining our efforts, weakening our faith, destroying our families and stealing our children's minds. In addition are the heavy spiritual battles that our country and the world are facing, as we watch moral relativism and attacks against Jews and Christians increase by the minute.

Therefore, if our Bibles lay on our desks at the end of the day, unopened, we become as vulnerable as an unarmed soldier. We become easy prey for the Enemy.

And as Lucifer finds us vulnerable and defenseless, we lose sight. We lose faith. And our Faith Bridge starts to collapse.

A Weapon to Defeat Compromise

"We are destroying speculations and every lofty thing raised up against the knowledge of God, and we are taking every thought captive to the obedience of Christ." 2 Corinthians 10:5

Imagine that the blueprint leading you in the construction of your Faith Bridge called for a special type of concrete. Imagine that in order to speed up the process, you decide to use an inferior product, which is about the same thing, but not exactly what was ordered by the Architect.

In the process of mixing concrete, imagine you leave a key component out. Or add something that was not supposed to be in the mixture.

Your decision to change the recipe just a bit will render a weaker final product. It won't last. It won't stand the test of time. It won't bear as much weight.

We call it compromise. It's an insidious enemy that permeated the Corinthian church of Paul's day when he wrote the tenth chapter of Second Corinthians.

The location of Corinth made it a crucial center point for the cultures of the East and West in Paul's days. Located between the Gulf of Corinth (Adriatic Sea) and the Saronic Gulf (Aegean Sea), Corinth became an important commercial and military center for the Roman Empire. It was also a major cultural center of the Greco-Roman world, hosting the bi-annual Isthmian Games, which began in 581 B.C. at the Temple of Poseidon. Then in 146 B.C., after a revolt against Rome, Corinth was destroyed and later rebuilt to become a Roman Colony where Roman soldiers retired. During the Greek reign in Corinth, the temple to Aphrodite rose imperially more than 1880 feet above the plain. Before it was destroyed by an earthquake that assailed the city around 150 years before Paul arrived there, more than 1,000 prostitutes were part of daily fertility cults in this temple.

A place filled with spiritual darkness.

A mesh of two ungodly cultures tangled the city where one of the first Gentile churches began. In the center of it all, one of the largest synagogues outside of Jerusalem hosted a large number of Jews. Many of them were new believers.

Of all the cities where Paul planted the first churches across the Roman Empire, Corinth was the place where he met the strongest opposition. The Corinthian church was factitious, prideful and rebellious, highly influenced by Jewish false teachers and by the sensuality surrounding the pagan city.

It was an affluent, ungodly society.

Christians were struggling to remain faithful to God's Word while living in the midst of much darkness.

Leaders were compromising the doctrines of Christ to fit their lust and pride.

Does that picture look familiar?

Although Corinth is no longer the prominent city of old, its spirit is alive and well today. And unfortunately, just as it did in the ancient empire, it continually spills its lies into the modern church.

Indeed, many teachers and preachers nowadays are compromising the truth of God's Word, by either omitting important doctrines from their teaching, or emphasizing self-help principles instead of God's truth.

It saddens me to realize that many Christians follow them, blindly accepting their half-truths and compromise. Worse yet, their compromise and feel good theology are leading many "truth seekers" straight into hell.

Their teaching soothes the wounds, but does not heal.

It pleases the crowds, but not the Father.

It's dangerous and it's spreading like wildfire.

"A little leaven leavens the whole lump." Galatians 5:9

Compromising God's Word is one of the worse threats for a Christian. Once we start interpreting it to fit out personal views, we allow Satan room to twist the entire truth of the Gospel. We can easily see that happening as certain teachers or preachers start by twisting the truth just a bit, only to end up completely disregarding critical doctrines such as salvation through faith in Christ alone.

Many churches omit the doctrine of salvation through faith in Christ alone from their pulpits.

The blood of Jesus has been wiped away and omitted from many songs.

A little leaven. A bad end result.

The church in Corinth was facing that same peril. Thus Paul, in his candid, prophetic way of speaking the truth, reminded them of who is behind every compromise and how to fight it:

"For though we walk in the flesh, we do not war according to the
flesh, for the weapons of our warfare are not of the flesh,
but divinely powerful for the destruction of fortresses. We are
destroying speculations and every lofty thing raised up against
the knowledge of God, and we are taking every thought captive to
the obedience of Christ." (2 Corinthians 10:3-5)

The first realization is that the war against the church is spiritual.

Satan has declared war against mankind in the Garden of Eden and there he pledged to stop redemption's plan. He failed. Jesus fulfilled God's plan on the cross. Ever since then, the message of salvation has redeemed people throughout the centuries. Satan cannot stop it and it infuriates him

Therefore, if Satan cannot defeat the message of the cross, he'll distort it.

If he can't stop us from proclaiming the Gospel, he'll help us proclaim just enough truth to pacify men's hunger for God, mixed with a whole lot of lies to keep them from actually receiving salvation. Or, to the believer, he'll feed us just enough lies to keep us from receiving God's best.

The second realization is that we possess the weapon to fight his lies.

The *machaira.*

We have the weapon that can "destroy any speculations and

every lofty thing raised up against the knowledge of God."

That weapon is God's Word. We must read it. Study it. Digest it.

We must take everything we hear into the light that shines from it.

We must push every thought and action through the grid — Does it contradict scripture … or support it?

Does it glorify God? Or men?

An Anchor for the soul in stormy seas

As he pulled a chair to sit beside me, his somber voice reflected the emotions clearly seen on his face. He had received an answer for something we've been long waiting for. Something that affected our family's plans and dreams. Something he and I had been praying for and patiently waiting. A promise wasn't kept. I saw the disappointment in his beautiful eyes.

Disheartened, my husband poured out words that I heard from myself many times before.

"I know God has a purpose for this. I'm just upset right now."

I prayerfully asked God for wisdom. His wisdom, not mine. He whispered, "Look down." As I lowered my eyes, I "saw" God's voice, underlined and highlighted on my open Bible on the table. "My ways are far beyond what you can imagine." (Isaiah 55:8)

I should have known the outcome, for God gave me that passage on that very week during my quiet time.

How many times have you muttered under your breath: 'I don't understand it, Lord.' How many times have you laid down at night, wondering — 'What am I doing wrong?' How often do you hear yourself saying, 'Why me, God?'

If you are alive and breathing, I know you have asked these questions before. You may have done so even today.

I'd like to share with you an interesting concept that God laid in my heart. It's pretty amusing, yet true: As we try to take matters into our own hands, instead of reaching out to God for help, He sees us as grasshoppers.

That's right, grasshoppers. I didn't say it — God did. I'm a visualist, so please bear with me.

In Isaiah 40, one of my favorite passages in the Bible (and inspiration for my ministry's name,) the prophet gives us insight into Israel's rebellious and doubtful hearts. In this beautiful prophetic passage, God promises victory to Zion.

God's messenger sees past the surface of our faith and into the depths of our hearts. We doubt.

We simply doubt the wisdom, power, strength and unfailing love of our God. We just do it.

I do it. You do it.

We see our dreams crumbling at our feet and we lose heart.

Someone wrongs us and we quickly wish to take matters into our own hands.

We receive bad news and we despair.

All the while, God is "sitting above the circle of the earth" while He sees us, below, hopping around.

Grasshoppers (v.22).

In the meanwhile, He "stretches the heavens like a curtain", "reduces rulers to nothing" (v.23), "calls each star by name…and does not miss a single one, naming all 10 sextillion (and counting) of them.

Our brains know that. But our hearts don't. When life happens, instead of anchoring our hearts on His truth, we keep on hopping.

Grasshoppers.

If we are to build a strong Faith Bridge, we must allow the Bible not only to be our weapon of defense, or the weapon to defeat compromise, but we also must allow it to become an anchor to hold us down when our lives are tossed about.

We must allow it to help us remember that God's love does not change.

When life tosses us about, we must ask ourselves: Do we really grasp God's love? Do we understand that "He (does indeed) work all things together for our good" ?(Rom 8:28).

Can we see God, sitting above it all, seeing past our present and into our future — what was and is and is to come.

Can we see the great Maestro, conducting the magnificent orchestra of our lives, comprised of instruments of all types, some carrying a beautiful tune, some pounding annoying and loud beats, all disconnected when played separately, but making a divine melody when He conducts them according to His perfectly composed sheet.

Do we grasp God's love and grace, poured into each page of His Word?

Perfect love displayed on blood-stained stretched arms on the tree. Do we? I dare say — we often don't.

Not with our hearts, at least.

That's why we must build a strong Twelve-Inch Faith Bridge, so that when our hearts tell us there is no hope, we tell it what God says in His Word.

I believe this is indeed one of the most important lessons to be learned by God's children, in order to be able to reach a place where circumstances will not alter how we see God, His love and grace.

He does not move. We do move, as well as our circumstances. The reaction of all humankind is the same. We hurt - we scream. We get scared — we doubt. These are natural, but not necessarily permanent, responses.

We must be willing to mature and go past our natural response to our circumstances and search God's heart to find His peace. We must be anchored in His truth, lest we miss the turn and get lost.

His Word is as good as He is

> *"The rain and snow come down from the heavens and stay on the ground to water the earth. They cause the grain to grow, producing seed for the farmer and bread for the hungry. It is the same with my word. I send it out, and it always produces fruit. It will accomplish all I want it to, and it will prosper everywhere I send it." (Isaiah 55:10-11)*

Man is ever quick to promise and slow to perform.

We all have been promised things that never come to pass, from the "I do's" that end in divorce to job promotions that never happen.

We are often so wrapped in man's natural type of thinking and acting that we forget, that although men are created in God's image, we cannot compare His faithfulness in fulfilling what He promises to ours.

God is like, yet unlike man.

We are indeed but faint copies of Him and He is altogether better than we. His Word (and therefore His promises), cannot fail. If we hold on to the truth and obey the commands, His Word will accomplish His perfect will for our lives.

But there is a catch

There is only one requirement for our Christian lives that needs to be fulfilled:

Stand in the center of God's Will

"And we know that God causes all things to work together for good to those who love God, to those who are called according to His purpose." Romans 8:28 (NASB — emphasis added)

The only "if" on Romans 8:28 and other scriptures which give us security of God's steadfast faithfulness is whether or not we love Him and are following Him — His instructions and His directions.

If you can honestly assess your life and to the best of your ability and honesty, you can say that you are His follower, not just His child, you can then rest in the fact that He is working on your behalf, even if your world is seemingly falling apart.

However, should you be living in deliberate rebellion, you won't be able to honestly claim Romans 8:28.

If that is your case, then, yes, you should really be hopping and fretting, for God cannot dwell in darkness and cannot speak to you unless you are near Him. As God sits above the circle of the earth and looks at your life, He cannot show you the next step in His perfect path unless He has your full attention.

Peace in the Midst of the Storm

Oh, that we may reach a place in our journey with Christ, where we are so enamored by His grace, so in tune with His plan, that our hopping around won't last long when trials strike.

Instead, we will be anchored in His truth, ready to handle our *machaira* against our enemy, using it to defeat every compromise.

Practice, practice, practice!

We hear it repeated by every coach, music teacher and moms and dads everywhere. One cannot master anything without much practice.

The same is true regarding handling this mighty Weapon we own. We must read it every day; we must quote it when we feel oppressed. We must teach its truth to our children and encourage them to journal the times when the Word speaks directly to their hearts.

The only way we will be able to successfully handle our mighty Weapon of War; the only way we will be able to use the Anchor to keep us steady in the raging sea is if we study it, know it by heart and apply it to our lives.

Jesus Himself showed us how to do battle against the enemy when He was tempted by Satan in the wilderness. Three times did the devil tempt our Lord. Three times Jesus used the *machaira* against the enemy. Quoting passages found in Deuteronomy and Psalms, Jesus sent the devil running with the power of God's Word. (Matthew 4:7-11)

Irresistible

Definition: too powerful or convincing to be resisted.

Synonyms: uncontrollable, overwhelming, overpowering, compelling, irrepressible.

To the world, God's word may be temporarily resistible. I say temporarily because we know that one day "every knee shall bow and every tongue shall confess that Jesus Christ is Lord" (Philippians 2:10). To the forces of darkness, however, His Word has always been and forever will be irresistible, overpowering, overwhelming.

A Christian who knows his or her Bible and uses it each day is dangerous to Satan; hence his fierce attacks! But if we handle our Bible as God intends, with authority and might, we can rebuke Satan's attacks and rest in the shadow of the Almighty's protection (Psalm 91).

As a Roman soldier would never enter into battle without his sword, I have decided long ago that I would handle my *machaira* every day, learning how to use it in order to find victory through each trial and battle. I listen to praise music throughout my darkest days, filling the air with God's truth.

The more I read it, study it and apply its truth to my life, the deadlier It becomes to the darkness I face.

It is my most precious possession. My weapon. My protection. my blueprint. My GPS.

Without it, we get lost. Our enemy overtakes us. Our Faith Bridge becomes weak and brittle.

Anchor Sticky Notes

Many years agoI developed a habit to write Bible verses on sticky notes or 3x5 cards that I post all around my house.

There are verses on my refrigerator, on my pantry door, on the window by my kitchen sink where I wash the dishes, on my mirror where I get ready every morning and around my computer screens.

I call them *Anchors* because that is exactly what they have become — anchors for my heart when I need to tell it how to feel.

Just as they are to ships in the midst of mighty storms, these anchors have become life savers to me. They can do the same to you.

The skies are getting darker

Satan is pushing hard in his last attempt to condemn the world to eternal death, rendering the church of Christ powerless and ineffective.

Everything around us is changing.

As the salt of the earth and light of the world, we cannot allow or afford him to change US!

Therefore, if we are to be victorious in our pursuit of strong faith, we must pick up our Weapon of war and handle it daily. Before you listen to me ... or to the most eloquent evangelists out there.... Listen to the Word.

Listen to *ho Logos*. The Word that became flesh to redeem you. The Word that is alive and speaking to you with the same power that it did 2,000 years ago when the Corinthians opened their second letter from their beloved leader.

Yes, listen to The Word.

Because the battle for your mind and for the lost souls is raging and you must take every thought captive in order to win it (2 Corinthians 10:5).

Chapter 10

The Power of Your Words

"With the tongue we praise our Lord and Father, and with it we curse human beings, who have been made in God's likeness. Out of the same mouth come praise and cursing. My brothers and sisters, this should not be." James 3:9-10

I was mindlessly browsing through a magazine at a doctor's waiting room when a national news alert popped up on the TV screen. A fire had started at a warehouse close to my hometown. The video showed the flames quickly devouring everything in their path. The program stopped for commercials and when it returned, I could see that the flames had spread quickly and seemed to be destroying a fortune in inventory at the warehouse. Black smoke covered the beautiful summer skies. The fire department's water hoses were obviously overcome by the fury of the fire. It would undoubtedly consume everything in its path.

The next day, the County Fire Chief reported that the huge fire was accidental. A spark from a metal that scratched the concrete floor initiated the huge fire that destroyed sixty five per cent of the company's inventory. One spark! The offender was one tiny, accidental spark.

If the apostle James were to summarize the central message of his book, I believe he would say,

"You know the truth, brothers and sisters. Now live it." His book is indeed filled with instructions on how to live in the Christian faith.

159

The third chapter addresses a crucial issue of which we must be aware, in order to build and maintain a strong bridge between our faith and our walk: *The Power of our Words.*

I once had a conversation with a mother who was suffering because one of her children did not visit frequently. As our conversation progressed, she told me some of the things she would say to her daughter during her rare visits. After hearing her words, I frankly understood why the daughter's visits were so far and between. When confronted about the way she spoke to this grownup daughter, the lady told me,

"I have the right to tell her whatever I like. She is my daughter and she must respect me. This is who I am". After hearing her, I couldn't help but imagine James nodding his head and saying in his straightforward, yet poetic manner, *"Wrong answer, ma'am! Our personalities and circumstances should not determine or justify what comes out of our mouths. Read my book."*

In the beginning of his third chapter, James reminded the reader that only a perfect man could have full control of his speech at all times. Since we do know that "there is not a righteous man on earth who continually does good and who never sins." (Ecclesiastes 7:20) then what are we to do? Should we just throw our hands up in the air and accept our unrestrained speech simply as part of who we are? Unfortunately, this is a very common reason used to justify our lack of control over our tongues and other fleshly behaviors and desires. But if we are to live out our faith, connecting what we know about our God to the way we live our lives, we must indeed learn to master the tongue.

James, the apostle of practical Christianity, compared it first to two familiar mechanical gadgets, then to one of the most powerful forces of nature. In each of the illustrations, he selected very insignificant-looking devices used to accomplish great results. The illustrations are very graphic and each one is more telling than the preceding one.

The Horse Bit — Help to Restrain our Flesh:

A horse is so strong and muscular, that the power in the engines of the fastest cars ever made is measured in horse-power. Yet, as regal and stout as this animal is, it is extremely unruly if left in the wild. However, by putting a bit in its mouth, men can practically have complete control over all its movements. Literally — the horse is controlled by its mouth. Likewise we, God's children, are able to bridle our whole body by subjecting our speech to the control of the Holy Spirit.

The wild horse in this example may have also been used to illustrate the passions of the flesh in their wild nature. Think of adultery, for instance. A flattering word spoken many times carelessly sometimes fuels the beginning of carnal desires that cause marriages to fail and families to be destroyed. Indeed, the person who is careful in using his speech may find it very useful to keep himself or herself from falling into destructive temptation.

The Ship's Rudder — Controlled Direction

The rudder is a small gadget located at the bottom of even the most majestic cruise liners. The unseen rudder is significantly small in comparison to the size of the ship, but it enables the steersman to guide a large vessel and sail it to its final destination. Not only does the rudder keep the ship in its course, its power can also help the vessel counteract the force of mighty winds and storms in the sea. The metaphor used in the second example shows yet another facet of the power of the tongue. It can steer our lives into the right direction or, if not used properly, it can so damage our destiny that we may find ourselves far away from where God purposed we should be.

Indeed, we could say that there is abundant life or death to a life of purpose in the power of the tongue (Proverbs 18:21). If we submit our speech to the power of the Holy Spirit that lives within us, the strong winds which often assault us as we sail to our destiny will not change the course of our lives. However, if we use our tongues to bring curse to our lives or to utter blasphemies against God, then we break the connection with that divine Compass Who would otherwise help us stay on track and fulfill His purpose for our lives.

Fire — Gossip and Slander

Fire is a powerful force of nature which usually starts accidently and then consumes everything in its path. Just as in the example of the flames that assailed the factory close to my hometown, fire which starts with a small spark can destroy a lifetime of work and memories. Thus the illustration used by James is purposefully very graphic to describe how damaging our words can be when we use them to slander our neighbor. His metaphor also leaves the reader with a strong sense of the ultimate origin of the motives behind destructive speech: Satan himself,

"And the tongue is a flame of fire. It is a whole world of wickedness, corrupting your entire body. It can set your whole life on fire, for it is set on fire by hell itself." James 3:6

Damage made by fire spreads far and wide, just like careless words can damage a person's character, hurt a child's self-esteem for life or severely damage a relationship. Sometimes a small comment or an angry word spoken hastily creates a wedge between husband and wife, the closest of friends, or parents and their children. Careless and wicked speech scorches and consumes: lies, gossips, slanders, profanity, curses — every time a child of God uses these evil words, we spit hell's fire into people's lives and as well as our own.

The Matter of Careless Words

There is also the fact that we are sometimes simply careless with words. It's not that our hearts are always full of hate, anger or jealousy necessarily; we may just be in the habit of using some words carelessly. We may only be caught up having a good time with friends and suddenly speak without thought. We may not mean any harm by something we say, but because we did not restrain our words, we ended up hurting someone.

In my country of origin, people tend to be point-blank when they speak. Brazilians are often fervent about their opinions and Latin languages are filled with passion in the way they express their feelings. So did I ever have a road ahead of me when I married an southern American gentleman! Many times I would come across as angry, when I was just trying to make a point clear. I wasn't angry and certainly did not mean to be hurtful. However, for the person receiving our words, perception is reality. My words and therefore my mood were interpreted and perceived as angry. I knew quickly that I had to become more attentive not to use words carelessly and with the wrong tone.

Jesus addressed the importance of careless words on the last verse of his conversation with the Pharisees in Matthew 12:

"But I tell you that EVERY careless word that people speak, they shall give an accounting for it in the Day of Judgment. For by your words you will be justified, and by your words you will be condemned."
(Matt 12:36-37)

This passage made me think about how I use my words. On the day I stand before my Lord, I shall give an account for every word I spoke, particularly the idle ones. According to the English scholar John Gill:

"In the original Greek, the word used for 'idle' means 'unprofitable talk', which, though it does not directly hurt God or man, yet is of no use to speaker or hearer; and yet even this, in the last general and awful judgment, if not forgiven, and repented of, must be accounted for." [1]

The Bottom line

"For the mouth speaks out of that which fills the heart. The good man brings out of his good treasure what is good; and the evil man brings out of his evil treasure what is evil." Matt 12:31-35

These words, addressed to the Pharisees by Jesus himself, are a stern reminder of the truth behind our words: often our tongue pours out what our hearts are filled with.

The Master's admonition should make us all shudder! It should make us rush to scan our hearts any time we catch ourselves saying something harsh or angry. Or any time that we find ourselves in the process of judging someone, gossiping or slandering. What are we really feeling? Could it be jealousy? Unforgiveness? Could it be that the person's behavior reveals a secret sin that we also struggle with? Regardless of our motives, Jesus' words don't change. Our tongues often pour out that which our hearts are filled with.

The Power of praise

"Therefore I will give thanks to You, O LORD, among the nations, and I will sing praises to Your name." 2 Samuel 22:50

Another aspect of utter importance when it comes to our speech is the power of praise. The Bible is filled with verses calling the saints to praise God. As we face hard circumstances, we must learn to deliberately praise Him, even when we do not feel like it, trusting Him to deliver us from each trial as He promises He will. Thankfulness opens the door to God's presence and is built on that frame of trust. Gratitude is heaven's language and we must learn to speak it at all times.

One of the usual misconceptions about praise and gratitude towards God is found in the reason we praise Him. Praise flows easily out of our mouths when everything is going well. But we find it hard to praise Him during our trials. Of course, as we face life's hardships, our flesh does not desire to be grateful. I believe that happens because we associate our praise and worship to the gifts we receive, instead of the nature of the Giver.

"God is not a man, that He should lie, Nor a son of man, that He should repent; Has He said, and will He not do it? Or has He spoken, and will He not make it good?" Numbers 23:19

The secret to endless gratitude is to change the praise paradigm within us. We must teach our hearts that God never changes and that He is faithful to keep His promises. We must tell ourselves that although our circumstances may not be good, God remains good. He is still the Giver of every good and perfect gift, even when we cannot see it (James 1:17).

God is still a good God, even when the world as we know it, is falling apart. The moment we accept this, we are able to start praising Him continuously.

That may just be the lesson to be learned in some of our trials.

Choosing to Speak Life

"I'm fat." "I can't get a job." "I can't do anything right!" "I'll never get out of debt." "Prince Charming is lost and can't find the way to the castle."

I repeatedly hear comments such as these coming from faithful Christians and have been guilty of declaring some of them myself. Poisonous statements that we often say without a second thought. Death and defeat that we carelessly speak into our own lives.

It may just be that we have grown up hearing them and therefore simply continue a "family tradition" of self-deprecation. Or it may be caused by insecurities and low self-esteem. Or it may just be a bad habit.

"From the same mouth come both blessing and cursing.
My brethren, these things ought not to be this way. Does a fountain
send out from the same opening both fresh and bitter water?
Can a fig tree, my brethren, produce olives, or a vine produce figs?
Nor can salt water produce fresh." James 3:10-12

Several messages and entire books have been dedicated to the fact that we can destroy a child's future with the words we send their way. Or to the fact that marriages would be restored if husbands and wives were more careful to restrain their tongues. But what about the blessings and curses that we declare upon our own lives with the words we use? James teaches us that our tongues have the power to alter our destiny: We cannot expect to reap figs if we plant vines. Likewise, we cannot expect to reap blessings if our tongues declare words of defeat into our lives.

In their book, *Words Can Change Your Brain,* Andrew Newberg, M.D. and author Mark Robert Waldman make a case for the fact that words can literally change your brain. They write, "A single word has the power to influence the expression of genes that regulate physical and emotional stress."

"By holding a positive and optimistic [word] in your mind, you stimulate frontal lobe activity. This area includes specific language centers that connect directly to the motor cortex responsible for moving you into action. And as our research has shown, the longer you concentrate on positive words, the more you begin to affect other areas of the brain. Functions in the parietal lobe start to change, which changes your perception of yourself and the people you interact with. A positive view of yourself will bias you toward seeing the good in others, whereas a negative self-image will include you toward suspicion and doubt. Over time the structure of your thalamus will also change in response to your conscious words, thoughts, and feelings, and we believe that the thalamic changes affect the way in which you perceive reality."[2]

Don't you just love when modern science confirms what God's Word has declared for centuries? Indeed, long before scientists were able to measure the effects of words and thoughts in our brain structures, God's messengers had already declared the result of negative words in our lives.

We can talk all day about the effect of negative words in our brain's frontal lobe or the positive effects of positive speech in our brain activity. But the fact of the matter is, You and I know that God is more concerned about the reasons why we may be self-destructive in our speech.

If you find yourself saying the same negative things over and over again, ask the Holy Spirit to reveal what is really in process.

Could it be that you don't feel worthy of God's love or that you have believed the devil's lies you heard repeatedly as a child? Could it be that you are connecting your worth with material or physical attributes and forgetting who you really are in Christ? Or maybe you are following your parent's footsteps of self-deprecation and defeat?

Whatever the reason, God is faithful to reveal it to you. More importantly, He is faithful to enable you to overcome it, in Jesus' Name! You need to choose to believe what God's Word says about you,

"You are beautiful. Accepted. Loved.

"You are able. Victorious. A Conqueror. Royalty !"

You have the river of truth running through you. Let the depth of its wisdom come out of your mouth. Let it bless you.

Chapter 11

Do Not Stall Progress!

"God knows our situation; He will not judge us as if we had no difficulties to overcome. What matters is the sincerity and perseverance of our will to overcome them." C.S. Lewis

We all have made them and we all have dropped them.

New Year resolutions are common in the western cultures. There is something about watching the old year slip away into the past. We feel like a reset button has been pushed and a sense of renewal and empowerment fills our souls. There is hope for the goals we did not accomplish in the past year and the tasks which have gathered dust, sitting on our ever-growing to-do lists. We watch the year come to an end and we make resolutions again — ones that hold the promise of a more fulfilling, organized way of life, better health or better finances.

However, like a child filled with excitement enjoying a new toy on Christmas morning, only to discard it a week later, we often play with our New Year's resolutions for a while, and then drop them when things don't happen as fast as we expected.

Statistics show that 40 to 45% of American adults make one or more resolutions each year. Losing weight, exercising and stop smoking are the top resolutions that half of the American population commits to once the Time Square ball hits the ground.

One week later, however, studies show that 25% of these

individuals have already dropped their resolutions. The number grows to 29% at the end of the second week and 64% after six months.

The result of our unwillingness or lack of will power to stick to our objectives leaves us with a sense of low self-esteem and the impression that the obstacles to accomplish our goals are bigger than the power within us and even God's power to enable us.

Extraordinary faith will not happen overnight. It takes time, effort and much patience, as we fight against our environment, personality traits, and (often) lack of will power.

My purpose in this chapter is to identify the issues that often make us stall our progress in the pursuit of strong faith and to offer you fresh perspective in order to keep on building your Faith Bridge.

Issue #1 — Identity Crisis

"But you are a chosen race, a royal priesthood, a holy nation, a people for God's own possession, so that you may proclaim the excellencies of Him who has called you out of darkness into His marvelous light." 1 Peter 2:9

One of the things we need is a fresh perspective regarding our nature as a child of God. In Chapter 13 of his book *Extraordinary,* John Bevere tells the tale of a price who was kidnapped at birth. For many years he lived with peasants, and was told that he was poor, a slave of sorts. One day the king's men found him and brought him back to the castle. Although he was royalty, when he awakened, he went to the garden to fetch his own breakfast. A chef cooked him a feast, but his old lifestyle was so engrained in his heart that he had a hard time living as a prince. Bevere compares this illustration to the way that we, God's children, tend to live:

"Each of us was born enslaved to the "ordinary". Now we must be liberated to think and believe "extraordinarily". Paul desires to "mend and make good whatever may be imperfect and lacking in your faith" (1 Thessalonians 3:10, AMP). If we believe we are no different than those who haven't been liberated by the grace of God, we'll live as they do — in the ordinary. We'll live the way we were trained, captives of this world's system. However, if we allow the Word of God to change how we see ourselves, and we truly believe it in our heart, then we begin to live like heaven's royalty — the realm of the extraordinary!"

It's about more than a list of do's and don'ts. It's about more than a list of places a Christian should or shouldn't frequent. It's a matter of appropriating, with all our hearts, the new nature that we have received as children of the King. It's more than saying we are His children. It's believing it and actually living it. It's bringing what we know to our hearts and allowing that knowledge to influence our walk. It's a brain-heart connection. A strong Twelve-Inch Faith Bridge.

As we take possession of our nature as children of the King, we realize that we have access to His resources, His presence, His table.

Furthermore, obeying becomes second nature.

Indeed, I'm afraid many Christians "fall from the bandwagon" because they allow their old lifestyles to influence their walk. They forget who they are; or, worse yet, they have never understood who they are in the first place!

Because they have not appropriated their position as children of the King, they end up going back to their old ways, often committing the same old sins and walking with the same old companies. Consequently, that of which they knew for so many years will certainly have a huge influence in their walk.

Therefore, one of the steps to remain strong in the faith is to allow our new creature to be nurtured, deliberately choosing to be separated from ungodly influences, until we become firm enough in our faith to indeed influence them rather than vice-versa.

Issue #2 — Paralysis

> *"And let us run with endurance the race God has set before us.*
> *We do this by keeping our eyes on Jesus, the champion who initiates*
> *and perfects our faith." Hebrews 12:1b-2a (NLT)*

I am fascinated by eagles. To say that the eagle is my favorite bird is an understatement. I developed an interest in eagles long before I became a Christian.

It started when my mom read a story about eagles and their ability to soar in the highest places, overcoming physical and environmental challenges. Mom was raised at a time and place where women were not allowed to accomplish much; therefore she has always challenged me to dare to fly high and reach places of which she could only dream.

I remember that any time I'd come to her with a "can't do" attitude, she would look at me with those fierce Spanish eyes and say: "Don't tell me you cannot do it before you try it and give it your best! You can do anything you set your mind upon, provided you work hard and do not allow fear to overcome you. You are my eagle!"

Although the thought behind this attitude were extremely valid, because I primarily trusted on my own abilities and resources, I would constantly feel helpless and disappointed when my efforts failed. Without God as a lighthouse to guide my journeys, I had collected a good number of shipwrecks by the time I was 25 years old.

"Yet those who wait for the Lord Will gain new strength; They will mount up with wings like eagles, They will run and not get tired, They will walk and not become weary." Isaiah 40:31

When I started life as a Christian, Isaiah 40:31 quickly became my life's verse. Mom's eagle stories became even more meaningful to me, as I realized how God uses eagle metaphors throughout Scriptures as a symbol of victory, perseverance and strength for those who trust Him.

As I started studying eagles, I found out that they soar by using thermal currents of air, which are warm air patterns created by the surrounding terrain. When they reach the right altitude, they spread their wings and their tail feathers and let the wind carry them to new heights, then they glide down to catch another upward thermal.

Soaring saves an eagle's energy, because it does not have to flap its wings as often.

However, in order to reach those currents, the eagle needs to first flap its wings and become airborne. The warm air patterns do not reach the ground or the rocks upon where the eagle rests. It must first do its part and start moving toward the currents of air which will sustain it and take it to new heights.

The same is true for every Christian. The Lord promises to sustain us just as the currents of warm air keep the eagles soaring; however, we must first flap our wings of faith, in order to reach the place where His power and strength take over.

The problem remains that many of us do not reach the place where we can soar with Him because we allow our problems or the influences of our environment to paralyze us. Therefore we become like eagles that are perched on the rocks, refusing to start the flight that will take us to the warm current of air which will help us soar above our circumstances.

Whatever you do — don't stop!

It was October 20, 1968. Thousands of spectators filled the Mexican City Olympic Stadium. Runners from all over the world endured a 24-mile, 385-yard event. Mamu Wolde of Ethiopia crossed the finish line, looking as fresh as when he started and won the gold medal. As other runners kept arriving in the stadium, the spectators started to get up to leave. Suddenly, the sound of ambulance sirens filled the air. All eyes turned to the gate as runner number 36, wearing the colors of Tanzania entered the stadium.

His name was John Stephen Akhwari. He hobbled with bloody, bandaged legs the entire 400-meter track to the finish line.

The stadium exploded in cheer and applause as the spectators watched the smile of triumph over pain that this small man displayed as he finished his race. Later that day, a reporter asked him: "Why did you continue the race after you were so badly injured?"

His sobering answer is an inspiration to my soul:

"My country did not send me 7,000 miles to start the race. They sent me 7,000 miles to finish it."

God did not save you and me so we'd start our race. He saved us so we would finish it and finish it well.

The problem with many of us is that we are easily entangled by our feelings. As storms hit our lives we often become paralyzed with fear and feelings of hopelessness. We allow our emotions to rule our thoughts and our overactive minds during all waking hours as we try to figure out how we can resolve our predicaments. Our injured and weary spirits give heed to the circumstances and to the enemy of our soul, which commands that our problem is too big.

And so, before we know it, we simply stop walking.

We become paralyzed and ineffective Christians.

Our Faith Bridge starts to crack.

I have witnessed numerous times where men and women of faith who were once giants for Jesus become as crippled soldiers, too tired to try, too worn out to stay in the race.

In the midst of our trials, God looks at us and says — *"Stand up, child! It's not over until I say it's over. You have a race to complete. You have a cloud of witness around you whom you are influencing with the way you respond! You must not quit! Flap your wings of faith that you may get to a place where my strength will make you soar; the place where I Myself will sustain you. But before you get there, you have some walking to do. You have a flight to start. You have work to do and a legacy due to keep your Faith Bridge strong.*

Stopping is not an option

But how can you continue in the race, when you are so tired? When your spirit is crushed? When everyone around you seems to be going the opposite direction from you? That's a good question.

I think we can start by addressing your thought patterns.

Living a victorious life is often a matter of perspective.

When troubles assail us and we feel like quitting, one of the keys to not stall progress is to change our perspective on our troubles.

And the Bible can certainly help us with that!

A Shift in Perspective

"For you, a thousand years are as a passing day, as brief as a few night hours. (...) Teach us to realize the brevity of life, so that we may grow in wisdom." Psalm 90:4,12 (NLT)

I was watching one of my favorite shows on the Animal Channel when the host of the show said, in his captivating British accent: "I am looking down from this mountain at this ancient valley, realizing that the rocks I'm stepping on are over 2 billion years old..."

Two billion years ... really? Wow! My mind cannot grasp that kind of time.

Let me make it clear that I don't mean to argue the age of the earth, although I personally believe that, if I understand my Bible correctly, science has the earth's age calculated incorrectly.

Nevertheless, my purpose is to debate the concept of time through God's viewpoint, the brevity of life and its time in light of eternity. The Bible clearly states that a thousand years for God is like a day or the few hours of the night (Psalm 90:4.)

In light of His infinity, even two billion years are but a blink. But for us, His earthly minded children, some days feel like a week, some weeks like a month, some years like — well, eternity.

Have you ever gone through a trial or a phase in your life, which seemed to last forever?

Maybe you are going through one right now ... waiting for true love, waiting to become pregnant, waiting for a job, waiting on God for healing.

Maybe you are waiting for something to stop or something to start.

Invariably, at some point in time or another, we catch ourselves watching the clock tick as we wait on God for different things.

Now — can you go back in your mind and recall a trial or situation that you experienced in the past, in which, when you were in it, it seemed like it would never end, but now, years after the fact, it seems like it happened decades ago?

I believe we all can.

Time — what do we, God's children, make of it?

Do we have the right perspective? Are we counting our years with a heart of wisdom, welcoming the lessons we learned, at whatever cost, or are we counting the years as the world does — by how much we do or don't have, by what we have accomplished and by desperately trying to reverse the signs of time that show in our aging bodies?

Psalm 90 certainly hit me with this question: How am I numbering my days?

It certainly seems to me like I turned 20 just the other day, but I have already doubled that count at the blink of an eye.

How have I lived these years? What have I done with time, while waiting for God's promises in my life? What am I learning about Him, as the trials I face often drag on for much longer than expected?

How am I using the time He gives me, one day at a time?

One hundred years from now

About two years ago I came across this coffee mug, actually meant for teachers, with the following quote on it: "What you do will matter one hundred years from now."

When I read that, it made me think of life, one hundred years from now. Although I don't know exactly what I will be doing, I do know two things about my life one hundred years from now:

Number One — I will be home in a place called Heaven, enjoying the glory of God.

Number Two — Whatever happened in my earthly life one hundred years before, will not matter to me by that time, at all.

It may certainly still be impacting the world I leave behind, but the troubles I faced here will certainly not follow me into eternity!

That thought gave me new perspective of how truly temporal life problems are. These will not matter one hundred years from now, when I am walking along the Crystal Sea, enjoying the presence and glory of God.

However, one thing will certainly matter:

How did I respond to life and its trials?

Heaven training school

Oh, that we may grasp this very true concept with all our might: that life is a school, a training ground for life eternal.

Life is the classroom for eternity.

If that's the case, shouldn't we take heed of Moses' prayer on Psalm 90, as he says "teach me to number my days, not wastefully or with things that do not matter, dear Lord, but help me to gain a heart of wisdom." (v. 12 paraphrased)

Shouldn't that perspective change the way we see our trials?

Shouldn't it make us have the strength to keep on walking, in spite of what we go through? I believe it should.

Moses' prayer in Psalm 90 craves God's teachings in every aspect of his life. This is the prayer of one who seeks to know the God Who gives us each day, and Who allows each trial, even though we often do not understand. This prayer reveals a heart that understands that life is not about us, but about God. It affirms that we are His students and as such, we need to pay attention to what the Master is teaching, submit to His instructions and acknowledge His much superior knowledge:

"For as the heavens are higher than the earth, so are My ways higher than your ways and My thoughts than your thoughts." Isaiah 55:9

Think about it: we are so quick to tell our children: "Pay attention to your teacher!", but how many times do we ignore the teachings of the Master ourselves!

Could this be the reason many times our "lessons" last for such a long time?

Could it be that we have not attained the answer to the problem yet and, like in math class, we must stay at it, until we learn?

Could it be that the lesson is not one that will benefit us as we anticipate, but, rather, it is a lesson of trust in the One Who holds our lives in the hollow of His hand and Whose thoughts about us are always for good, not ever for evil?

The One who promises He is with you always, no matter what? We often read and quote Jeremiah 29:11, but listen to God's words in the following verses (12-14):

"For I know the plans I have for you, says the Lord. They are plans for good and not for disaster, to give you a future and a hope. In those days when you pray, I will listen. If you look for me wholeheartedly, you will find me. I will be found by you, says the Lord."

Start the count today

How does the right computation of our days lead to applying our hearts to wisdom?

Because it makes us aware the transience of this life and how unworldly we need to be as Christians.

Think little of the world's riches and glory

How much would it matter for a prisoner who has been given a death sentence to know that he was left a fortune?

Not much at all! In Luke 12, Jesus tells a parable about a self-centered farmer in Luke 12 thought that he had it made! He had a very productive land and labored to make more room for more possessions. He tore down his barns to build bigger ones. He kept his mind on earthly riches and glory and thought he had planned wisely, after all, he had enough to last until his old age. He said to his soul: "Eat, drink and be merry". But the truth was: He did not even have a tomorrow. God said "You fool! This very night your soul is required of you and now who will own what you have prepared? So is the man who stores up treasure for himself, and is not rich toward God". Luke 20-21 (NASB)

Think Little of life's troubles

If we apply the "one hundred years from now" concept, we realize how truly brief our problems are, in light of eternity.

I know this is easier said than done, and I don't claim to understand the suffering in everyone's trials. However, I've had a share of hurt and pain and I can say that any time I get my focus off of my pain and into the vastness of God and His goodness, His promises, and His power, I get new insight into my problems.

I challenge you to do the same.

Whatever are your experiences, weigh the blessings you have and then God's promises to you on the other side of the scale. I am confident in this — if you are one of His children, your scale will always tilt towards the good if you look through the lenses of faith and into eternity.

Try it. That exercise will surely give you strength to take another step. And then another.

Think of life's troubles as an opportunity for eternal gain

Paul reminds us of how our troubles, if seen through God's eyes, shall produce imperishable fruit for our souls: "For our present troubles are small and won't last very long. Yet they produce for us a glory that vastly outweighs them and will last forever!" 2 Corinthians 4:17 (NLT)

As I look back in my life and I realize how fast it is evolving, I am challenged to count each day of the next half of my life on earth, with a heart of wisdom.

I am challenged to focus my eyes on one hundred years from now and review whether or not I am mastering the lessons of Heaven's training school.

I want to be in the honor roll of the Master.

I want to receive my crown with a smile from the Teacher, as He says "Well done!"

I want to have a "crowd of witness" behind me who were impacted because I walked the walk, as well as talked the talk. I want to impact them because I finished my race, no matter what.

One hundred years from now, when I am strolling on the streets of gold, I want to be able to see faces of people who my life touched for His glory. For this is the ultimate lesson of this training school — to live in a way that people around us will want to know our Jesus because of how we lived our lives.

"Therefore, since we have such great a cloud of witnesses surrounding us, let us also lay aside every encumbrance, and the sin which so easily entangles us, and let us run with endurance the race that is set before us, fixing our eyes on Jesus, the Author and Perfector of faith, who for the joy set before Him endured the cross, despising the shame, and has sat down at the right hand of the throne of God." Hebrews 12:1-2

Issue # 3 — Perfectionism

Perfectionism …
If you are a woman, I guarantee you've been jealous of a perfectionist.

I know it well. A recovering perfectionist, for many years I struggled with thoughts of inadequacy and failure. I strived for straight As and dreamed of straight hair. Perfectionists were usually raised by a perfectionist parent and therefore their tendency to strive to be the crème de la crème in everything they do is usually a cry for love and acceptance. Unfortunately, unless they recognize the issue, they carry on the legacy to the next generation, unintentionally pushing their poor children into the same trap.

Perfectionism is another reason why many people stall progress in their objective to build a strong Faith Bridge. They make mistakes and give up. They fall into temptation again and they think they cannot live the Christian life. They see others accomplishing more than what they do and start comparing their gifts and talents with other people's.

It's not an easy trap from which to escape. But if we want to have an abundant life, if we are to build a strong Faith Bridge, escape we must!

We can start by reminding ourselves of this truth: That God is not impressed by our performance. He wants our all of hearts and souls. (Deut 10:12).

Hearts that understand that our perfection is only found in Him (Ephesians 2:8-10).

Hearts that make His will our priority.(Psalm 18:30)

Hearts set less in seeking perfection and more in perfecting our love and devotion for Him. (Psalm 51:10)

Indeed, today I realize that perfectionism is the world and Satan's way to make me rely less and less on God and more and more on fallible, inadequate, me.

Instead of attaining perfection, the result will always fall short of our target: We become stressed out, needy of approval, self-indulgent, impatient. Simply hard to deal with.

And worse yet, we give up. We stall. We lose sight. We lose faith.

Through the Grid of God's Grace

Our good work and great performance should be viewed through the grid of God's grace. By grace we are lavished with opportunities, gifts and talents which allow us to do our best and be our best.

As Dallas Willard said "Grace is God acting in our lives to do what we cannot do on our own."

Indeed, God never designed us to accomplish perfection without him. He never designed us to build our Faith Bridge in one day ... or on our own!

Changing our perspective in life makes you keep in the race

"Choose to view life through God's eyes. This will not be easy because it doesn't come naturally to us. We cannot do this on our own. We have to allow God to elevate our vantage point. Start by reading His Word, the Bible ... Pray and ask God to transform your thinking. Let Him do what you cannot. Ask Him to give you an eternal, divine perspective." Charles R. Swindoll

We were again in the midst of a financial dilemma.

I had lost my job and we were living on one income. God had clearly told us that I was to stay at home and turn my dedication to raising our children and developing my writing career.

I looked at a blank computer screen as the cursor blinked at me. My brain was as blank as that page. My thoughts, all over the place. I had been sick and medical bills were piling up.

I turned around and let the sun shine on my face as I sought His face ... "I need fresh perspective, Lord!"

As the sun shone on my face, a flood of new perspective filled my soul:

No, my 401K portfolio is not nearly close to what it needs to be for retirement; my children's college savings plan looks pretty skimpy at the moment. Our van has more miles than the trail of tears and we have spent many vacation days around our hometown. Still, I realize, we are lavishly, wonderfully rich.

I have learned that an abundant life is indeed a matter of perspective.

I know many people who have much more than we do and who are so very poor.

Then there are those who will never have anything or do anything of much consequence in life because they don't believe they can. Faith believes that which we cannot yet see, and the key to success in life is to fully trust that fulfilling your God-given dream is just a matter of time. It is also to cherish and to be grateful for the things you do have.

Indeed, trust and thankfulness are a powerful team.

But as basic as these concepts may seem, they are often not easily grasped in real life.

We cannot easily count all of the examples of people who overcame adversity. These are great men and women in history who became successful not because "destiny" handed them a fair share, but because they fixed their eyes on their goal and would not quit until they arrived at their destination.

Winston Churchill, Anne Frank, Helen Keller and Nelson Mandela. These are only a few of the people whose names are forever engraved in the list of "Unforgettables" because they each had a vision, saw beyond their circumstances and never stopped believing.

What changes our perspective in life is the same for all of us —
we look at our circumstances and become fearful and paralyzed. We
hear the word cancer and we think death. We lose our job and our
hope walks out the door. We anchor our worth on things, situations
or on our performance instead of trusting the amazing, all powerful
grace of a God who deeply loves us and who wants the best for us.

As we fix our eyes on the storms and uncertainties of life, we
forget that the problems we face do not define who we are and
certainly do not determine our future, but the way we handle the
storms and uncertainties are directly related to our faith and beliefs.

Regardless of how old we are, our story is not over until we
draw our last breath. When asked about success, Michael Jordan's
statement was a sober reminder of the key to success: "I have missed
more than 9,000 shots in my career. I have lost almost 300 games.
On 26 occasions I have been entrusted to take the game winning
shot, and I missed. I have failed over and over and over again in my
life. And that is why I succeed."

The next time you look at your circumstances and feel tempted
to quit or get discouraged, I challenge you to take a step back and
broaden your view. As if through the scope of a camera, open your
lenses wide and zoom out of your problem. Take a second, honest
look into your life. Count your many blessings. Take a nature walk
to view God's faithfulness to the birds and the flowers.

Sing a song of praise.

Next, grab a firm hold of your vision. Your dream. God's
promises. Above all, even if you are hurting, just keep on walking.
And never give your problems more power than what they have.

Remember that God honors those who trust in Him- those
who work diligently to fulfill their purpose in life and never give up.
Make yours an unforgettable story of strength, faith and success.

Chapter 12

Connecting to Service

"Use the talents you possess: the woods would be very silent if no birds sang there except those that sang best." Henry Van Dyke

There is a burning desire in the heart of the surrendered Christian to make an impact in the world through their gifts and talents. We can't expect to be an effective member of the body of Christ if we stand alone on the sidelines. He who gave Himself completely to us, requires that we too become servants in His kingdom.

"Keep on loving each other as brothers and sisters. Don't forget to show hospitality to strangers, for some who have done this have entertained angels without realizing it! Remember those in prison, as if you were there yourself. Remember also those being mistreated, as if you felt their pain in your own bodies." Hebrews 13:1-3 (NLT)

It's Not About You

I call it the belly button syndrome: we all suffer from it from time to time. Some of us are chronically ill with it. We get so caught up in our own little world, our own problems and issues, that we forget that there is a world out there which not only is hurting, it is dying every day without Jesus. We don't even have to go that far. Our churches and small groups are filled with people who are hurting worse than we are.

The last piece in building our Twelve-Inch Faith Bridge is service. Christians who reach a place where their faith matches their walk will be eager to serve others with their talents and gifts. Mature Christians exude selflessness as they humbly serve those who are in need. Serving takes our eyes out of our problems and fills our hearts with purpose and joy.

Connecting to Service

Indeed, serving is a crucial part of a life of faith. I actually learned the joys of serving and using my talents to help others long before I became a Christian.

I was only ten years old when I started teaching.

We will call her Mary. She was our live-in maid. She was only sixteen and had been raised on a farm, the daughter of a poor farmer who had no means to take his children to the nearest school. When I found out Mary could not read nor write, determination filled my heart - my friend would not remain illiterate! So I talked to my mom, who was a teacher. She gathered the materials we needed and Mary and I started on a journey together.

Every day after school, I would finish my own homework and we would move to our "classroom" in Mary's quarters. We would open up the books and I would proudly write on the chalkboard, slowly unfurling a brand-new world, filled with excitement and hope for Mary.

I don't remember the entire process and surely cannot tell you how we did it, but by the end of six months, Mary could read and write. Within my heart, much beyond pride, a new passion was born. I was going to be a teacher. And teach I did, for the next several years, starting at the age of fourteen, when the language school where I studied English as a second language invited me to become one of their staff. That started a journey that went on into my young adult years and into the beginning of my days as a Christian.

But surprisingly as it may seem, it took me sixteen years after becoming a Christian to realize that God wanted to use my talents as a teacher and communicator in His kingdom.

"As each one has received a special gift, employ it in serving one another as good stewards of the manifold grace of God." 1 Peter 4:10

It started in 2006. As I shared in the introduction of this book, I was pregnant with our younger daughter when I came across Jesus' words on John 10:10 — "I came that they may have life, and have it abundantly." These words pierced my soul as the truth about my spiritual life surfaced: I was not living the abundant life! Oh, I was going to church and would read my Bible … some. But there was a longing inside me that revealed that there was more to life than what I was experiencing.

The fire that ignited my spirit when I first surrendered to Christ was not burning as it once did.

It was then that I started to ask God to show His plan for my life and how to use my talents and spiritual gifts to further His kingdom. That's when the content of this book started to grow in my life.

For the next three years, I dug deeper into the Word, learning more about God and His ways. And as I drew nearer to God, I started feeling a strong longing to serve Him in some capacity. I just didn't know exactly where to start. I prayed that He would reveal what He wanted me to do for Him. I even asked three of my closest friends to pray for me, so strong was the impression that I was missing His calling for my life.

For a long time, two years to be exact, my prayers for revelation continued to come back unanswered. Inside me, there was the certainty that something was missing; that there was a special purpose for my life that was as yet to be uncovered.

If you are a Christian and you have a strong desire to be used by God, but don't know where to go or what to do, if you have an uneasy feeling within your heart, as if you were missing something important, let me suggest that I firmly believe that if God is calling you to serve Him in some form or fashion, that you will have no real peace and joy until you find your place of service in His Kingdom.

Several people have shared with me that they feel the Lord's nudging them to serve Him and that they are not sure exactly what they need to do or where to start. If that sounds familiar, I know exactly how you feel and although I evidently cannot tell you what God is calling you to do, I can guarantee you this: the longing in your heart is for a reason and you should not dismiss it. From personal experience, I would like to suggest some of the things that I believe could be the reason or reasons as to why we sometimes cannot figure out exactly what God is saying to us when it comes to ministry.

Patience . . . It may not be the right time yet

"So let's not get tired of doing what is good. At just the right time we will reap a harvest of blessing if we don't give up."
Galatians 6:9 (NLT)

We are bound by elements which do not limit God, such as time and physical boundaries. When it comes to His plan for our lives, He often must move pieces and position them in the right places, so we can prosper in what we are called to do. This moving and changing takes time. As painful as it is to wait, we must remember that God is not just propping up His feet and maliciously making us wait. He is always at work.

"For from days of old they have not heard or perceived by ear, Nor has the eye seen a God besides You, Who acts in behalf of the one who waits for Him." jhkv, Isaiah 64:4

Since your ministry will usually involve other people, resources and the right opportunities, you must remember that, while you wait, God is positioning the right people, resources and opportunities for you. He may be working in the hearts of those who will come alongside with you, preparing them for their roles. He may be moving resources in order to provide the financial means you will need. He may be changing hearts (including yours) to be ready for whatever sacrifices that may need to be made.

Remember that, while you wait, it is a perfect time to get to know Him better. It is a great time to get to know yourself better, to learn more about your spiritual gifts and talents, as well as to make an honest assessment of your limitations.

That brings me to the second reason, why I believe, it often takes us longer to hear from God.

Something may just have to go!

"And He was saying to them all, "If anyone wishes to come after Me, he must deny himself, and take up his cross daily and follow Me. For whoever wishes to save his life will lose it, but whoever loses his life for My sake, he is the one who will save it." Luke 9:23-24 (NASB)

As soon as I started to feel the Lord nudging my heart into serving Him in a ministry capacity; He started dealing with me concerning a habit.

For a long time, I thought that the uncomfortable feeling that came along with this habit was unfounded; after all, I honestly did not believe it was a sin. Regardless, the uncomfortable feeling would not go away and the closer I walked with the Lord, the strongest the discomfort became. One Sunday, Pastor and Author Andy Stanley was preaching as a guest at our church. He preached on the story of Esau.

We all know that this strong hunter gave up his own inheritance for a cup of soup.

Old news … Sad story. I thought to myself: "I've heard this sermon before."

Was I ever wrong! Andy Stanley has an amazing gift for finding new nuggets in old, well-known passages of Scripture. He asked us to turn the Bible to Matthew 1, the genealogy of the Messiah. And there we read:

"The record of the genealogy of Jesus the Messiah, the son of David, the son of Abraham: Abraham was the father of Isaac, Isaac the father of Jacob, and Jacob the father of Judah and his brothers." Vs.1,2

That is when Andy stopped, looked at the congregation and said: "Do you realize that this verse should read: Jesus the Messiah, the son of David, the son of Abraham: Abraham was the father of Isaac, Isaac the father of Esau?" Because of a cup of soup, Esau gave up the inheritance that would record his name for eternity in the lineage of the Savior of the world."

Messiah!

He then turned to the audience and said: "What is your cup of soup?"

In that moment, God spoke loudly to my heart. It was not about right or wrong, sin or not sin. God was saying to me: "Will you lay it down?"

It was about obedience.

Was I going to justify or obey, even though I did not understand? I chose to obey. I laid it down.

Two weeks later, God revealed to me that I was to teach and write. Soaring with Him Ministries was born. Blind obedience was the last step He expected of me before revealing His plan for my life and ministry.

There may just be a habit (or sin) that is preventing the Spirit from freely working in your life.

If you are reading this example and something keeps popping up in your mind, please do not dismiss it. There is a reason for the discomfort. God loves you and wants to use you, but something may just have to go. It may be a habit, like gossiping or judging. It may be that someone in your life has hurt you and you need to forgive them. Whatever it is, God is making you uncomfortable for a reason. He cannot use a dirty vessel or an unwilling spirit! His work requires sacrifice of things we love and it certainly requires a heart that is willing to be molded and changed.

As hard as it sometimes is to change or give up things which are dear to us, the blessing and joy that are only found when you are in the center of God's will far exceed any pleasure in life.

You must take that first step

A second reason as to why God may not yet have revealed His calling for your life is if He told you to take a small step and you've been ignoring Him.

It may have happened when your church announced that the children's ministry needed workers, and you felt compelled to sign up, but never did.

It could be that you felt compelled to participate in an informational meeting about short term missions in your church, but dismissed it, because you felt inadequate.

It may be that your heart fills with joy when your church's choir or praise team sings, but you have decided you cannot add another commitment to your schedule. Whatever is nudging your heart, dismissing it is like telling God that you are not willing to sacrifice or, by being afraid, you are denying the unlimited power of God, which can enable you to do anything He calls you to do.

If God calls you, He will reveal it to you. If He reveals it to you, He will show you if anything in your life needs change. If He shows it to you, He will give you the strength and courage to obey. When you are ready, He will guide you step by step and will enable you. However, He needs you to say yes and take the first step of obedience.

I urge you not to waste another day.

God will not reveal His entire vision for your life. If He did, He might just overwhelm you. As you take one step at a time, He will reveal His plan for you and send the people and resources you'll need to accomplish your calling. I know He will. I've seen it done.

Don't hold back because of fear or feelings of inadequacy.

When God revealed to me that I was to write and speak to women in America, I thought about Moses. I could completely relate to him and his feelings of inadequacy. When God told him to go speak to Pharaoh, he felt the weight of his handicap pressing on his shoulders:

"Then Moses said to the LORD, "Please, Lord, I have never been eloquent, neither recently nor in time past, nor since You have spoken to Your servant; for I am slow of speech and slow of tongue." Exodus 4:10

When God told me that I was to write and speak to women, in

English, my second language, that's exactly how I felt.

"What about my accent, Lord? People may not understand me. I don't have an English degree! I'm not a writer! I'm not even from here!"

But God didn't see my handicap. He saw His omnipotence.

And He saw my surrendered heart.

The rest is history.

"But God has chosen the foolish things of the world to shame the wise, and God has chosen the weak things of the world to shame the things which are strong, and the base things of the world and the despised God has chosen, the things that are not, so that He may nullify the things that are, so that no man may boast before God."
1 Corinthians 1:27-29

God has opened doors of which I have never dreamed. I have a column on the largest newspaper in the Southeastern United States. I've been invited to speak to American audiences in many places. This book manuscript was only rejected three times before being accepted by my publisher. (Anyone who's written a book and tried to publish it knows how unlikely to happen that is.) My devotionals are now translated into two other languages and are now featured on the iDisciple app, with over 120 million subscribers. All this happened after a simple yes to obedience and to the first step He showed me to take.

I can't claim any of it. Like Moses, I often feel weak, inadequate, small. But that's when I'm reminded that my God is unlimited, omnipotent and all-knowing. My inadequacies become tools that He uses to amaze the world. If I can do it, anyone can.

I pray you take courage in that truth.

I am not telling you that it will be easy. When you are called into ministry, rest assured that you will be tested and tried. You will go through fires, valleys and hardships. You'll find out who your true friends are. And it will hurt.

But I can guarantee you this much: when you are doing God's work, there is a joy and peace that you will find nowhere else, regardless of your circumstances.

I can speak with the experience of someone who has known professional achievement in the secular world. However, I can honestly say that never in my life have I found more fulfillment than since I took a step of faith and said yes to the ministry God has called me to do.

There is something about doing God's work in this fallen world that fills a gap in your heart like nothing else will.

Moreover, when the last chapter of your life is over, it will not matter what title you held, what you drove, where you lived or the size of your portfolio. We all know you will not take any of that with you. But what you did for Christ - that will forever remain and continue to impact the world after you are gone.

Think about it: If He used a tiny stone in David's sling to bring down the giant; if He used Moses' willing hands to open up the waters of the Red Sea, there is no question that He can use you.

But the question is, are you ready and willing?

Another important question I must ask you is: are you plugged into a church? Better yet: are you plugged into the right church, where your knowledge of God and faith can grow and your gifts and talents can be used?

Church — "To go or not to go- that is the question"

I could not resist it — I had to amuse you with a small twist of William Shakespeare's famous opening line of Hamlet's third act. In that monologue, Hamlet struggles with whether or not he should kill himself because of the events that had depressed him greatly. I can't help but think of some Christians I know who have stopped attending church regularly.

Many of them have stopped maturing in the faith. Others feel discouraged, defeated and even depressed. Others are living meaningless, worldly lives. I truly believe that "To go or not to go" is a matter of (spiritual) life or death for all Christians. It is in the church that we are taught in the "more excellent ways" of God (1 Corinthians 12:31). It is there that we can expect to feel uncomfortable when confronted with sin. It is there that we have the optimum opportunity to use our spiritual gifts to further God's kingdom on earth.

"Not forsaking or neglecting to assemble together [as believers], as is the habit of some people, but admonishing (warning, urging, and encouraging) one another, and all the more faithfully as you see the day approaching." Hebrews 10:25 (Amplified)

We can't expect to be an effective member of the body of Christ if we stand alone on the sidelines. God has called us to assemble and be instructed in His Word:

"The body is a unit, though it is made up of many parts; and though all its parts are many, they form one body. So it is with Christ".
1 Corinthians 12:12 (NIV)

But where's a good church?

Often, the right question to the Christian wishing to grow in love, devotion and knowledge of God is not whether or not to go to church. Rather, it is where to go. The church should not appeal to you as a mere social club and it should not be a place where we only seek to be entertained.

So how do we know where to go? I'd like to suggest some of the things that should be considered when choosing a home church.

Prayer

The first thing a Christian should do is to pray and ask God to show him or her where they should attend. God is willing and will show His children the congregation where they will be more effective. There are many wonderful churches out there, but there will be one that will feel like home to you. As you visit churches that your friends attend or close to home, ask God to reveal where you should attend. He certainly will!

Preaching

If you're looking to become effective as a mature Christian, it's important that you're plugged into a church whose pastor believes the Word of God in its entirety. There should be no room for compromise. A good pastor preaches from the Word of God and doesn't omit any of its truths. Indeed, God could not be any clearer regarding His disgust for those who add or cut the content of His Word. It is amusing to me that He left that instruction spelled out on one of the last verses before He closes His revelation to the church. Hear God's somber word to those who "add and cut" from His Holy Word:

> *"I testify to everyone who hears the words of the prophecy of this book: if anyone adds to them, God will add to him the plagues which are written in this book; and if anyone takes away from the words of the book of this prophecy, God will take away his part from the tree of life and from the holy city, which are written in this book." Rev 22:18-19*

I'm also very skeptical of pastors whose sermons are filled with self-help and feel-good theology.

Of course a pastor must exhort his flock and encourage them with the wonderful promises in the Word of God; however if his preaching never leaves you convicted of sins; if his teaching does not make you eager to know God in a deeper way, I would say, "Keep looking!"

"

For the word of God is living and active and sharper than any two-edged sword, and piercing as far as the division of soul and spirit, of both joints and marrow, and able to judge the thoughts and intentions of the heart." Hebrews 4:12 (NASB)

Missions

A Bible-teaching church will be a giving church. This church will be highly involved in missions and will call you to get involved in missions in some fashion, whether by going, praying or giving. The Great Commission was not an option for Christ's disciples. It was a commandment from Christ Himself:

"And Jesus came up and spoke to them, saying, "All authority has been given to Me in heaven and on earth. Go therefore and make disciples of all the nations, baptizing them in the name of the Father and the Son and the Holy Spirit, teaching them to observe all that I commanded you; and lo, I am with you always, even to the end of the age." Matt 28:18-19

The Dangers of an Unfruitful Life

If we are to build and maintain a strong Twelve-Inch Faith Bridge, if we want to experience the abundant life that Christ promised His followers, a fruitful life is not an option. It is a necessity. Serving is another key element in building strong faith. Furthermore, an unfruitful Christian life is a dangerous one. Jesus told a parable to illustrate God's viewpoint regarding the fruit that His children should bear and the danger of an unfruitful life:

"A man had a fig tree which had been planted in his vineyard; and he came looking for fruit on it and did not find any. And he said to the vineyard-keeper, 'Behold, for three years I have come looking for fruit on this fig tree without finding any. Cut it down! Why does it even use up the ground?' And he answered and said to him, 'Let it alone, sir, for this year too, until I dig around it and put in fertilizer; and if it bears fruit next year, fine; but if not, cut it down.'" Luke 13:6-9

As a little girl, I would count down the months until summer each year. I lived in the city and spent every summer vacation at my grandmother's farm by a salt water bay. I have many fond memories of those days; most of the happy memories involved the freedom we had and the abundance of fresh fruit and fish available at arm's reach.

I remember sitting down below a fig tree and resting under its shadows with my cousins. We'd reach up and get a juicy fig for a snack. I still remember how flawless and tasty they were and I can even recall the scent of this perfect fruit. Interestingly enough, that fig tree was neither planted in any special place nor was it tendered by anyone. It was actually on the side of a dirt road, in the middle of nowhere, standing alone.

Planted in good soil, the tree was bearing good fruit. I dare say that the small road that ran beside the tree was built around it, so that the fruitful tree would not have to be cut down.

In contrast to my childhood's fig tree, the one described in Luke 13 is tendered by the Vineyard-Keeper, loved by Him, and still remains barren for years. The parable is a picture of Almighty God in His dealings with His children. The Man (Owner) is Jehovah God. The vineyard is His kingdom — the realm of God's truth and righteousness that He has been establishing on earth through His people since His covenant with Abraham. Israel and the gentile believers are the fig tree, which God planted in His vineyard. Jesus is the Vineyard-keeper.

Notice that this tree has been planted by the Owner, not by chance, but by design. This is you and me. A fig tree in a vineyard. An odd tree seemingly in the wrong place, different by Divine Design and unfortunately, fruitless by choice:

"And he said to the vineyard-keeper, 'Behold, for three years I have come looking for fruit on this fig tree without finding any. Cut it down! Why does it even use up the ground!" v.7

The three years mentioned in the parable are significant. The number three in the Bible stands for completeness. Israel was given chance after chance to redeem itself in three different phases of its history: (1) By the Law, (2) By the Prophets (3) By Christ. And still, as the Owner comes looking for fruit of repentance and change, He finds a tree with no fruit. Thus still fruitless, the tree is not only on the way — it's taking space of other trees that would otherwise bear much fruit in God's kingdom.

Not only is it fruitless, it is a bad influence to the world around it that is watching it. It must be cut down.

God does come to each of us for His harvest. When He comes, what will He find?

"My Father is glorified by this that you bear much fruit, and so prove to be My disciples" John 15:8

The tree in the parable is alive. It draws enough substance from the ground to keep it from dying — it draws the moisture away from the surrounding soil and receives the rain and sunshine from Heaven. This tree is not a reference to a non-believer, stranger to the blessings and abundance of God's grace, provision and love. Rather, this tree exemplifies the believer who, received nourishment and provision from God and still bears no fruit and doesn't seek to serve others.

The tree receives, however it does not share. It is fed, but does not feed. This is a Christian who is ministered to, but does not seek to minister to others. This is the Christian who has gifts and talents, given by God, but is just sitting in the pews, seeking to "be blessed". This is also a picture of the Christian who is holding on to sinful habits and life-style, keeping one foot in the world and one in the church.

God cannot and will not effectively use him or her.

I am writing much on my own experience. As I mentioned before, sometime after my salvation, I let the passion for Christ that had once engulfed my entire life, cool down in my heart. And so there I stood, at the corner of the vineyard, bearing little fruit, sharing little, being nourished but not giving — keeping the gifts that God had given me within the self-serving sphere of my life and my relationships. I did not understand the uneasiness within my spirit at that time, the impression that something very crucial in my life was missing. Now I know: the Owner of the Vineyard had given me His sentence: CUT-IT-DOWN!

I don't know about you, but I know several Christians who can relate to my story — living in defeat other than enjoying the victorious and abundant life that Jesus promised. I am absolutely not referring to faithful Christians who go through difficult valleys. As I have explained on Chapter 7, the valleys are part of our journey and it is in them that we have the opportunity to grow closer to the Father.

I am talking about people who are living empty lives, portraying negative behaviors and defeated attitudes, even when everything is going well.

I firmly believe that the uneasiness and emptiness is often the weight of the sentence that God is giving: "CUT-(HE OR SHE)-DOWN.

Cut them down from My Peace, cut them down from My Guidance, cut them down from true fellowship with Me."

Thus we see these faces every day, going through the motions, reciting the right verses, singing along songs of praise. But ultimately, their peace and joy is skin deep. No wonder! Living on the inside of these fellow Christians dwells the Holy Spirit of God, who is ready and willing to enable them to be what God designed them to be, but is being hindered by the person who is not willing to serve or to surrender his or her life completely.

One more year. Grace — once again.

In the parable, as soon as the sentence is pronounced, the Vineyard-Keeper (Jesus) pleads with the Owner (God): "One more year! Have mercy! Let Me fertilize it, dig around it and if it still does not bear fruit, cut it down!"

Under Christ's merciful care, God allows us another period for repentance, reformation, for renewal of heart and life. This is a sacred opportunity for His children — one that we must not neglect. May we heed His voice and search our hearts, for if we don't, the word of Divine condemnation will be spoken and we will lose our place of blessing in the Kingdom of God.

I would like to dismiss any misunderstanding regarding

salvation. I firmly believe that, once saved, God cannot cut you down from His eternal gift of salvation. The Bible is filled with verses to support this truth (John 10:27-29; John 6:37; John 10:28; John 5:25; Romans 11:29; 2 Corinthians 1:22 –to name a few). Indeed, salvation is a gift that cannot be lost. However, your deliberate disobedience and neglect to be used by God is certainly an invitation to remain fruitless and miss out on the awesome abundant life that Christ has died to give you. There is more to life and to eternity than just seeking to be blessed and ultimately going to Heaven. Eternity begins the moment we accept Christ as our Savior. Our journey to eternity begins with repentance and will be crowned with our faithfulness to His Word and the works we perform here on earth for Him.

What fruit do you have to show the Grower? Does your life reflect the joy and peace that comes from being in the center of God's will, even in the midst of the hardest trial?

If you were to be honest about your life, could you say that you bear fruit and that you offer shade for the people who are around you?

Do you know your spiritual gift(s)?

Are you praying and asking God to show how He can use your gifts for His glory?

Are there things that you are holding on to, because they are too dear to you, but which could be a stumbling block if someone were to seek your guidance and help?

If so, my friend, I urge you to surrender your life before His throne. Find what your spiritual gifts are; pray for discernment, give up whatever is keeping you from being all God designed you to be.

I promise, you will experience a peace and joy that is greater and better than anything this world can offer. You will feel a sense of completeness and you will be effective as you have never been before.

The blessings that are poured down when we choose to say yes to God are unlimited! You will discover gifts and talents that you did not even know you had! Moreover, when the Grower comes again to inspect His vineyard, your life will bear beautiful fruits for His glory.

He will smile at you and say "Well done, good and faithful servant. You were faithful with a few things, I will put you in charge of many things; enter into the joy of your Master." (Matthew 25:23)

The ultimate prize of serving others in the Name of Jesus is incommensurable: to know that your life is being used to change someone's destiny ... or to help a brother or sister in need of love and direction on this side of eternity; those are "the treasures in heaven ... where neither moth nor rust destroys, and thieves do not break in or steal." Matthew 6:20

Conclusion

Continuous Maintenance

"Watch your thoughts for they become words. Watch your words for they become actions. Watch your actions for they become habits. Watch your habits for they become your character. And watch your character for it becomes your destiny. What we think, we become. My father always said that ... and I think I am fine." Margaret Thatcher

Almost nine years. That's how long it's been since I stared at my Bible, wondering how to find the abundant life that Jesus had promised me on John 10:10. Nine years since I started to realize that there had to be more to life that living in a roller coaster of emotions, feeling joy one day and depressed the next. Nine years since I started realizing that strong faith is more than a gift from God, it is also a deliberate personal pursuit. Nine years since I embarked in the process of bridging the gap between how I feel and what I know about my God.

Nine years since I started on the journey to build my Twelve-Inch Faith Bridge.

Wouldn't it be great if the process was an easy one? Wouldn't it be wonderful if we could just do steps 1-2-3 and boom! We'd have a functioning, ready and strong Faith Bridge.

However, much like any construction on earth, whether it's a building or our Faith Bridge, there will need to be constant vigilance. It will need continuous maintenance. We must ensure that it withstands the mighty storms of life and also the weight that the world presses upon us, with its lures and traps.

My purpose in this conclusion is to show you that the process is never over. My purpose is to encourage you to commit to continually watch your words, actions, habits and character to ensure that your Twelve-Inch Faith Bridge remains strong. Likewise, we must remember that, as with any process of changing old habits, it will take time, endurance and discipline for our hearts to get to a place where we are able to instinctively "bridge the gap between how we feel and what we know about our God."

We won't wake up one day as champions of faith. I've been a Christian for 20 years and it's taken me that long to get to a place where I know the steps I must take in order stop my emotions from ruling my life. And I certainly know I'm not done. I just know the process. I've proven it true and effective. You can, too.

Margaret Thatcher's father taught her a principle that is all over scriptures. Watch-your-thoughts. If we don't, we open the door for an avalanche of bad decisions and ultimate defeat. At the end of the day, a strong Twelve-Inch Faith Bridge is a process of mind over matter, thus the importance of spending time with God in prayer and not only reading, but deeply studying His Word. The more we know Him, the more our hearts believe Him. The more we believe Him, the more we are able to fight the lies of the devil and the world. And if there ever was a time in history when we need to be more certain of what Truth really is, the time is now. Our world is filled with relativism these days and a Christian who is not sure of what he or she believes is doomed to be sucked into the trap of believing everything is fine and that God accepts anything.

He indeed accepts us as we are, but He never meant for us to stay the same. As Paul wrote to the saints in Rome, a place very similar to our current society:

"For those God foreknew he also predestined to be conformed to the image of his Son, that he might be the firstborn among many brothers and sisters." Romans 8:29

"To be conformed," he said. It's not magical. It's a process. God has predestined us, dreamed of having us become more like Jesus. We can't do that and remain who we once were, drenched in the filthiness of our flesh.

"Be Holy", He says throughout Scriptures.

It's a choice.

"Be patient, trust me." He says throughout His Word.

You can tell your heart to trust. And wait. You can make choices that will help you stay pure.

It's a choice. If you can only grasp that, you're in for an awesome start.

In order to be able to do be conformed, you must be ever on alert. Ever vigilant. Because trials will continue until the day you die. Temptations are not overcome overnight. The tempter knows your weakness and he's not bound to ever give up turning you into a fruitless, mediocre Christian.

I'd like to start talking about maintenance regarding our prayer life.

Be on the Alert for Spiritual Static

The radio host had my attention. The subject was intriguing. His arguments, passionate and compelling. I had been listening to the interview for about 15 minutes, waiting on a particular session of the program. After the commercials, the host continued the interview and asked his guest the question I was waiting to hear. I turned up the volume and inclined my head towards the speakers.

The next thing I heard was a sequence of squeals and squelching noises, erasing any chance of understanding the much anticipated answer. I turned the radio dial back and forth, to no avail. When the program was finally audible again, the interview had ended. Radio static had filled the air, preventing me from understanding the most important part of the interview.

Have you ever felt the same way in your spiritual life? You may be eager to hear His voice and directions, and yet, all you hear is … static. Random thoughts invade your mind. Uninvited silence permeates the room. You yawn, feeling sleepy all of a sudden. Rather than God's voice, you hear different sounds.

Frustrating, huh?

Spiritual static is a reality to every Christian. At some point in time during our journey with God, we all have had moments when we seemed to have "lost connection" with the Father. Many times, it merely means that God is silently waiting for the right time to reveal His plans. Other times, He is just in the business of quietly loving us. During those moments, His silence does not frustrate us. Our heart seems to know it — God wants us to enjoy the silence of His loving presence.

However, there are moments when our prayer time is filled with a lack of peace and unrest. Rather than silently enjoying His presence, I feel like getting up and starting my day.

Can you relate? Indeed it is tempting to dismiss this disconnection and go on with life as we know it. But we shouldn't. As a matter of fact, what I have learned is that it is during those times that I need to raise the red flag and search my heart. Something is amiss. The connection was lost.

Invariably, when the interruption in communication is followed by lack of peace, I am the one to blame. Jesus admonished His disciples about the dangers of not obeying His commands when He said:

"Why do you call me, 'Lord, Lord,' and do not do what I say? As for everyone who comes to me and hears my words and puts them into practice, I will show you what they are like. They are like a man building a house, who dug down deep and laid the foundation on rock. When a flood came, the torrent struck that house but could not shake it, because it was well built. But the one who hears my words and does not put them into practice is like a man who built a house on the ground without a foundation. The moment the torrent struck that house, it collapsed and its destruction was complete." Luke 6:46-49 (NIT)

Indeed, whenever we experience spiritual static during our prayer time, the best thing to do is find a quiet place and ask God to show us what is preventing us from hearing His voice.

It could be that, like David before repenting, we have unconfessed sin. It may be a blunt sin that keeps us enslaved to immorality or addiction. It could also be sins of the heart, those subtle emotions that we allow to take root in our lives, affecting everything, including our relationship with Yahweh: Feelings of pride, envy, hatred, unforgiveness, among others. As we discussed in a previous chapter, these little monsters become strongholds that create huge waves of spiritual static until we identify them and allow God to exterminate them for good.

But there is a more subtle culprit. This spiritual static ally can infiltrate our hearts without us realizing it: Delayed obedience. That is what I was guilty of when silence and unrest filled my prayer time not long ago.

I was feeling uneasy for several days. Spiritual static filled my prayer time. I finally decided to get to the bottom of it. As I retreated to pray, openly searching my heart for any hidden sin, I honestly could not find anything. Yet, I had the intense feeling that God wanted to show me something.

And so He did.

Several weeks before, God had given me a couple of tasks, which, quite honestly, I did not want to carry out. Using busyness as an excuse, I kept avoiding the subject day after day and procrastinating obedience. "I'll do it", I thought, "just not today." That morning as I prayed, God showed me exactly what He thinks of delayed obedience. He reminded me of how I feel when I ask our daughters to clean their rooms once, twice or three times over, without success. I had a vision of their messy rooms and the frustration and anger that rises up each time they don't follow through with their given tasks.

That's when I realized ... how can the Father show me the next step, if I do not complete the small tasks He gives me? God's commands are not optional. I was disobeying Him.

There will be days when you'll certainly feel like you lost the connection with the Father. You'll feel like your prayers hit the ceiling and bounce back. I suggest that in those days, you ask God to show you if there's something that He wants you to do and that you are fiercely avoiding.

I promise — He will show you.

Be on the Alert for the Holy Spirit Warnings

We visited Sea World in Orlando for the first time this past summer. It was time for Shamu's fantastic show at the end of a busy day. I sat towards the top of the stadium and watched, amused, as people ran up the stairs, dragging their bags, cameras and crying babies. Some had an awkward smile on their faces; others looked surprised to have found themselves completely soaked. Still others did not seem to have found much entertainment in getting wet.

I glanced at the opposite side of the arena and realized the seats that were so coveted before the beginning of the show sat empty now. Shamu and her friends had put on their best fin forward and indeed drowned everyone sitting on the first twenty rows of the stadium. I'm not sure which part of the show was more amusing: The killer whales' pirouettes or the diverse reactions of their soaked victims.

The people who ran away from the wet seats may have had different reactions to Shamu's playful performance; however they all had one thing in common: They were all warned in advance that they would get wet.

"Soak Zone", the signs cautioned.

Yet, as you watched their countenance while running away from the water range, you would have thought they had no idea it was coming.

That amusing sight made me think of how we often react to the Holy Spirit's warning signs.

I can go back to many "first impression" moments in my past and realize that I missed the "You're about to get soaked" sign countless times. Can you relate?

It may have been that person you should have never befriended.

Or the guy you should have never dated.

It may have been the business deal you were not comfortable with...

Or that strange feeling on the pit of your stomach telling you to back off...

Over and over again have my first impressions proven right. And yet, I dismissed them several times in the past.

"But when the Father sends the Advocate as my representative — that is, the Holy Spirit — he will teach you everything and will remind you of everything I have told you." John 14:26

When Jesus asked the Father to send us the Helper, we received the most amazing life tool anyone could ever ask for. It's a mighty tool, indispensable in the construction of a strong Twelve-Inch Faith Bridge.

The Holy Spirit is indeed our Helper as we navigate through life's trials and make difficult decisions. It is the Holy Spirit who comforts us when we are hurting and guides us to discern and understand the Scriptures.

But there is another very important assignment that this amazing Friend was given.

He is also the voice that warns us when we are about to get in a dangerous or compromising situation. Because He is God's love and God's knowledge, He knows exactly where each path we take will lead us. And He is always there to show us where to go … and which situations and places to avoid. As Charles Spurgeon masterfully explains in his book "Holy Spirit Power"[1]

"There is no man born in this world by nature who has the truth in his heart. There is no creature that was ever fashioned, since the Fall, who has an innate and natural knowledge of truth."

And as he continues, later in the chapter:

"The way of truth is very difficult. If you step an inch to the right, you are in dangerous error, and if you swerve a little to the left, you are equally in the mire. On the other hand, there is a huge precipice, and on the other hand, a swamp. Unless you keep to the true line, to the width of a hair, you will go astray. Truth is a narrow path indeed."

And the Holy Spirit's role is to guide us into all truth.

So, whenever you feel that uneasiness in the depth of your soul about a person, a place or a decision you are about to make, I dare you to stop. And before you choose to disregard the "Soak Zone" sign, remember that the Holy Spirit knows exactly what you will find when you get there.

There is a reason for the lack of peace. It's not intuition. Not if you are a child of God! It is God the Spirit, warning you that there is danger or unpleasant circumstances ahead.

Remember: It is the peace that surpasses all understanding that is the "GO" sign. Don't move unless you have that.

"And the peace of God, which surpasses all comprehension, will guard your hearts and your minds in Christ Jesus." Philippians 4:7

I'd like to call your attention to another dangerous element that often creeps in as we start maturing in our faith, especially when God's calling for our lives becomes clear and we step out on faith to serve in some type of ministry. The danger behind this particular element is that it creeps into our lives without external signs. It's a heart issue.

And heart issues are the most deadly.

Pride — Powerful Corrosion Element

"Humility is the mother of all virtues; purity, charity and obedience. It is in being humble that our love becomes real, devoted and ardent. If you are humble nothing will touch you, neither praise nor disgrace, because you know what you are. If you are blamed you will not be discouraged. If they call you a saint you will not put yourself on a pedestal." Mother Teresa

Teresa of Calcutta, born Anjezë Gonxhe Bojaxhiu and commonly known as Mother Teresa, was an ethnic Albanian, Indian Roman Catholic nun. As I read about this famous figure of the 20th Century, in spite of some controversies regarding her wavering faith through the years, one trait has stood out as rock-solid in her life — Teresa of Calcutta was humble.

She founded several orphanages and food banks, dedicating her life to reaching those who were hungry for food and love.

I grew up watching her pop up in the news quite often. A small-framed, frail-looking lady with sad eyes and a wide smile. The spotlight followed her, but she never seemed to care about being in it. She loved Jesus and wanted to be His light to the hurting, whether people clapped in approval or not.

As I ponder about Mother Teresa's ministry and the humility in which she gave, I am challenged to search my own motives when it comes to serving. Why do I do what I do?

Whether standing in the choir loft on Sunday mornings or speaking to women in conferences and retreats, whether giving to missions or sending a card to a hurting friend, I need to remember to keep my heart in check for signs of pride. We all do.

Jesus' words in Matthew 6 remind me to give and serve for the right reasons: out of love for God and our fellowmen.

"Be careful not to practice your righteousness in front of others to be seen by them. If you do, you will have no reward from your Father in heaven. So when you give to the needy, do not announce it with trumpets, as the hypocrites do in the synagogues and on the streets, to be honored by others. Truly I tell you, they have received their reward in full." verses 1,2 (NIV)

Heart religion

According to Jesus, religion is worth nothing until it becomes heart religion. That concept was often a focal point of His teachings during His three-year ministry. Heart religion says that more important than the outward expressions of faith, is the condition of one's heart.

Indeed, during the famous Sermon of the Mount, Jesus took sins such as adultery and murder to a new level, explaining that these are heart sins: If one hates his neighbor, he commits murder. If one looks at a woman (or man) lustfully, he or she commits adultery (Matthew 5). But as much as we must watch to keep our hearts from stumbling by avoiding these "heart sins," the Lord warns us in these verses about another dangerous enemy of true worship — hypocrisy.

He calls it the "leaven of the Pharisees" in Luke 12:1. He certainly was not too kind in regards to the condition of the Pharisees' hearts when it came to worship and service. Several times did Jesus call them hypocrites. In order to receive the applause and approval of men, these leaders would chose to "give alms" in the synagogues and in the streets, where there was a greater number of spectators to applaud them.

There is nothing wrong in giving in public — it is acceptable and routine to most Christians. It is the reason why we give and serve that must be sifted through. We must give because we love God and wish to obey Him and because we know that giving (whether we give our resources or service) is the heart of true religion: "Pure and genuine religion in the sight of God the Father means caring for orphans and widows in their distress and refusing to let the world corrupt you." James 1:27

The Heart of Giving

"Do not withhold good from those who deserve it when it's in your power to help them." Proverbs 3:27 (NLT)

Giving is in the heart of the Law of Moses and Christianity. Throughout the Bible, God encourages His people to be givers — of their resources and talents. Whereas salvation is through faith in Christ alone, a person who is truly surrendered to Christ cannot help but give. There is a burning desire in the heart of the surrendered Christian to make an impact in the world through their gifts and talents. Giving and serving satisfy that.

However, we must remember that the reward behind all that we do in the Name of Christ is lost if it is done for our own glory and vanity. Oh, what a chilling thought to ponder, that much of our service will be forgotten by God, if and when our true motives are far from giving Him glory. As Matthew Henry explains in his commentary:

> *"How many times service is rendered in the name of Jesus, but not from principle of obeying God and glorifying Him, but to satisfy one's pride and vainglory?"*[1]

Jesus' take on the matter is (as usual) direct — "truly I tell you, you have received your reward in full." (Matthew 6:2) In other words, Jesus is saying: "Enjoy the applause and the pat on the back (from men). Heaven will not remember."

May our "spiritual antennas" be ever alert to the lures of pride, lest we miss the blessings and true reward from God.

The Antidote

> *"Though the LORD is on high, he looks upon the lowly, but the proud he knows from afar." Psalm 138:6*

Something happened not long ago on a Sunday morning that grieved my heart. As I watched the situation unfold, God opened my spiritual eyes to realize how easy it is to be deceived by Satan while serving. God whispered in my spirit, "Many people serve me for the pleasure of being seen." I'll be honest. My first reaction was to jump right in and judge the person. "We should be here to serve God, not our pride," my heart cried out. "Shame, shame!" I thought. But when God put His Holy mirror in front of my face, I bowed my head, convicted.

Who has never done it? Who has never felt pride in receiving the applause of this world? I believe we all have at some point in time while serving God. That is human nature. It feels good to be loved and admired.

But if we are to be strong in the faith, if we want to continue to walk in a manner worthy of whatever calling God has for us, we must be ever aware that pride is a trap that Satan uses to make our service ineffective and without a holy purpose.

If you give in to the slightest prideful thought in regards to your service in the kingdom, Satan will snare you into thinking that the results of your ministry are due to your "amazing" talents and abilities. And before you know it, God will turn His face and favor away from your ministry. Because the truth is - we may reap the benefits of what we do for Christ; and we certainly will receive rewards for what we do in His Name. But the glory, oh, the glory, my friend, belongs to Him and Him alone.

Because I understand the dangers behind a prideful heart, and how it can certainly negatively affect our faith, I would like to share with you these simple "antidote to pride" steps. If you follow them, you are sure to keep prideful thoughts far from your heart:

Step #1: Search Me, O God!

"Search me, O God, and know my heart; Try me and know my anxious thoughts; see if there be any hurtful way in me, and lead me in the everlasting way." Psalm 139:23-24

Pray that God will expose the true reasons why you serve — is it for His glory? Is it to further His kingdom? Or is it to satisfy a prideful desire to be seen, admired, useful? If you ask the Lord to reveal it to you, He certainly will. As He does, ask Him to forgive you and help you focus your ministry on bringing Him glory, that you may truly worship Him in spirit and in truth. (John 4:24)

Step #2: Thank Him for closed doors!

"Worthy are You, our Lord and our God, to receive glory and honor and power; for You created all things, and because of Your will they existed, and were created." Revelations 4:11

Remember that God is who created all things, including your ministry. When you are fully aware of that truth, you will be able to give Him glory for the open doors, as well as accept the closed ones.

Remember that He is who calls us into service. If you are not chosen to perform a particular task, it is because God has something else in mind for you. Humbly accept and thank Him for the closed doors. If your heart is in the right place, you will develop a holy awareness that you are doing what God wants you to do and that, when He wants you to serve Him at some capacity, HE will move heaven and earth to accomplish His will for your life. Therefore … Do. Not. Strive!

Step #3: Refocus!

"We are destroying speculations and every lofty thing raised up against the knowledge of God, and we are taking every thought captive to the obedience of Christ." 1 Corinthians 10:5

Once you are aware of your weakness, do not let your guard down!

Satan will not give up alluring you into thinking that your success depends on your gifts and talents. You must be committed to take every thought captive on an ongoing basis, reminding Satan that "Every good thing given and every perfect gift is from above, coming down from the Father of lights, with whom there is no variation or shifting shadow." James 1:17. Indeed, we are empty vessels without Him!

Serving God with our talents and gifts is one of the most fulfilling things in life. I have found joy, contentment, peace and purpose as God opens doors and uses me to proclaim His Name.

My prayer to each person that reads this book is that you may become committed to give glory to the Giver of every good gift, every time you take center stage.

May we remain humble and grateful with the realization that God uses broken vessels like us to bring others closer to Him.

May we serve God in a way that when people watch us, they may see past our many flaws and have a glimpse of God's grace. May we realize each day, that as the audience applauds; they do so because Jesus is in the house and because He is the power behind anything we do or say.

"May I never boast except in the cross of our Lord Jesus Christ, through which the world has been crucified to me, and I to the world." Galatians 6:14

As we approach the end of this book, I'd like to call your attention to one more element that cannot be neglected in our walk of faith. This element has the potential to destroy our Faith Bridge.

Underestimating our weaknesses

"For all that is in the world, the lust of the flesh and the lust of the eyes and the boastful pride of life, is not from the Father, but is from the world." (v.16 — NASB)

I felt a bit like a school girl when our leader announced that Mandisa was part of our group. I didn't recognize her, sitting quietly at the corner of the small room.

"Oh, this is going to be good," I thought. "Now I will have to speak in front of ten seasoned speakers AND Mandisa."

I looked at the door and was tempted to run for it. That's when our leader told us that Mandisa was going to be part of our group, but as one of the participants. She was there to learn too.

Since that day last in the Summer of 2013, I have made it a point to follow her on Facebook and Twitter, and have encouraged my girls to download her music to their IPods. My older daughter went to her first Christian conference last month and had the opportunity to see Mandisa in concert. She was impressed by her music, but most of all, by her personality and transparency on stage. She shared "Overcomer", her newest album, which I've since heard a million times, as my girls twirl around the house, dancing to its tunes.

In January of 2014, Mandisa took my admiration of her work and personality to a new level. "Overcomer" won the Best Contemporary Christian Album and Song of the Year in the Grammy Awards. I did not watch the show, but found out about the win on her Facebook page.

As her name was announced, Mandisa did not walk towards the stage to receive the statue. Instead, she was miles away, at her house, watching the Award ceremony on live streaming. Naturally, the question started popping all over the Internet: Why did she choose not to be present for the ceremony?

In a Facebook post from January 27, 2014, she explains the reasons as to why she chose not to go. They are all very good reasons, but one in particular stood out as I read her post:

"Finally, the fourth reason I chose not to attend this year: yes, both times I have gone to the Grammys I have witnessed performances I wish I could erase from my memory, and yes, I fast forwarded through several performances this year; but my reason is not because of them, it's because of me. I have been struggling with being in the world, not of it, lately. I have fallen prey to the alluring pull of flesh, pride, and selfish desires quite a bit recently. (...) I knew that submerging myself into an environment that celebrates those things was risky for me at this time. I am taking steps to renew my mind to become the Heavenly Father-centered, completely satisfied with Jesus, and Holy Spirit-led woman I felt I was a few months ago, but I'm feeling a bit like an infant learning to walk again on shaky legs."[3]

I paused and smiled. Her entire post is inspiring, but this last part takes the cake. It made me think of how easy it is for anyone to fall prey to the alluring pull of all-things-flesh. We are called to be in the world, but not of the world (John 15:19). We were chosen to be light in the darkness, but often let the darkness around us dim our light. That's a dangerous, dangerous enemy of our Faith Bridge. Mandisa humbly recognized it and chose to pull away for a season of renewal and refocus.

I admire that.

Anyone can fall. We have seen it in the lives of prominent figures in the entertainment industry, people who were raised in church. We have witnessed it in the lives of several church leaders, pastors, as well as common folks like you and me.

"How did it happen?" we ask. I believe the answer is simple:

It happens one small decision at a time.

"Do you not know that a little leaven leavens the whole lump of dough?"
1 Corinthians 5:6b

223

The appeals of the flesh are near us every day. The devil has an army dedicated to luring the saints into temptation, compromise and ultimately, defeat. Unfortunately, too many of us fall into the deception that a little bit of this or that will not harm anyone. What a lie! Truthfully, a small step is all it takes to enter the road that leads us away from God's best. One tiny decision and years of building a strong Faith Bridge can be lost.

We must be very aware of that.

There is a reason I choose to stand in a place of no gray areas, where everything looks either black or white when it comes to God's Word.

I've been labeled as overprotective of my children and narrow-minded in my beliefs. I guess for all worldly standards, indeed I am. That hat fits me and I prefer it that way.

Why?

Because I am not so foolish as to think that falling into Satan's deceitful traps of compromise is beyond me.

As a Christian, I lived for many years dangerously spreading my feet between the Rock and the unsteady ground of old habits and compromises. That position left me, well, out of balance, so to speak. My Faith Bridge? It became terribly cracked.

It will do the same to you, or anyone, for that matter.

I believe that maintaining a worldly lifestyle creates a divided mind, a confused heart and a life filled with double standards.

In order to be the light of the world and the salt of the earth, we must let God's Word define and strengthen our boundaries, so that we are able to maintain them. His Word leaves no room for moral confusion. Right is right. Wrong is wrong. Our flesh will often be drawn towards sin. We must know our weaknesses in order to recognize when we need to draw back, regroup and refocus.

So here is a good question to ponder: Do you feel attracted to worldly things? Is there something that you know is a weakness, a temptation or stumbling block in your life?

If something comes to mind, it may just be a good time to follow Mandisa's brave example and take a step back out of the environments that are influencing you.

Maybe it is time to refocus and ask the Father to strengthen and guide you, so that when you do step into the world (as we are called to do), you are able to effectively and irresistibly shine Jesus' light to those who are trapped in darkness. Better yet, you'll be able to maintain a strong Twelve-Inch Faith Bridge.

"For you were formerly darkness, but now you are Light in the Lord; walk as children of Light." Ephesians 5:8

Some Last Words

Friend, *Twelve Inches* is not a magical book, guaranteeing an abundant life to all who read it. The tested and proven lessons in these pages, however, if applied, will help you reach a place where your emotions will not control your destiny any longer.

God has never promised to withdraw all trials, temptations and weaknesses from our lives. But He left us a blueprint, perfect directions to follow. He gave us His Spirit and we can count on Its guidance, each step of the way.

You know the life I started pursuing in 2006? The abundant, victorious life Jesus promised us?

I found it.

I found it in the midst of cancer.

And while mourning the death of a loved one.

I found it after losing possessions.

And when friends abandoned me.

I found it.

If you choose to follow my steps, listen to the lessons God has taught me in my walk of faith, I promise: You'll find it too. It won't happen overnight. Finding the abundant life in Christ is a process. A process that you must choose to follow, one day at a time. One challenge at a time. One blessing at a time. It will always need to be your personal, deliberate choice.

Paul knew it well. He found the abundant life too. In his letter to the Philippian church, he told them the secret of His contentment:

"Not that I speak from want, for I have learned to be content in whatever circumstances I am. I know how to get along with humble means, and I also know how to live in prosperity; in any and every circumstance I have learned the secret of being filled and going hungry, both of having abundance and suffering need. I can do all things through Him who strengthens me." Philippians 4:11-13

His secret? Staying focused on Christ. When in pain, he told his heart to trust His Savior. When in need, he did the same. When life was beautiful, he still focused on Messiah. He kept telling his heart to trust his God every day, until he got to the place where his circumstances did not destroy him:

"We are afflicted in every way, but not crushed; perplexed, but not despairing; persecuted, but not forsaken; struck down, but not destroyed." 2 Corinthians 4:8-9

The same will happen to you: Tell your heart what you know about your Maker, Redeemer and Savior. Tell it about His omnipotence, omnipresence, faithfulness and amazing, grace-lavished love.

If you tell it over and over again, your heart will believe it.

And you'll know that your heart has grasped the lessons contained in *Twelve Inches* when you attain joy, contentment and fulfillment, regardless of your circumstances.

Because those are the fruits displayed in the lives of those whose hearts are anchored in Jesus. In the lives of those who build and maintain a strong Twelve-Inch Faith Bridge.

Bibliography

Introduction
1. Barna Group, "Barna Survey Reveals Significant Growth in Born Again Population," March 27, 2006, https://www.barna.org/barna-update/article/5-barna-update/157-barna-survey-reveals-significant-growth-in-born-again-population.
2. John Bevere, *Extraordinary: The Life You're Meant to Live* (Colorado Springs, CO: WaterBrook Press, 2010).

Chapter 1
1. James Strong, *A Comprehensive Strong Dictionary of the Bible*, Logos Bible Software.

Chapter 3
1. Antidepressant revenue 2010 reference from the American Psychology Association: http://www.apa.org/monitor/2012/06/prescribing.aspx
2. Craig Groeschel, *The Christian Atheist: Believing in God but Living as If He Doesn't Exist* (Grand Rapids, MI, Zondervan, 2010), 52, 137

Chapter 4
1. Wikisource reference on John Donne's Meditation VXII: http://en.wikisource.org/wiki/Meditation_XVII

Chapter 5
1. Video from Purple Feather, Online Content Specialists: http://purplefeather.co.uk/#3
2. New American Standard Bible - 2 Corinthians 4:17

Chapter 6
1. Blaise Pasqual, *Pensées* (London, England, 1966)
2. Lysa Terkeurst, *Made to Crave: Satisfying Your Deepest Desires with God, Not Food* (Grand Rapids, MI, 2010), 129

3.   Samuel Taylor Coleridge, *Table Talk of Samuel Taylor Coleridge: And The Rime of the Ancient Mariner,* Christabel, &C (London, England, 1884), 94

4.   Charles Stanley, *Emotions: Confront the lies. Conquer with Truth* (New York, NY: Howard Books, 2013), 118.

Chapter 7

1.   Matthew Henry's Commentary on the Whole Bible – Logos Bible Software (Ecclesiastes, Chapter 3.)

2.   *Streams in the Desert, 366 Daily Devotionals* (Grand Rapids, MI: Zondervan, 1997), 365

Chapter 10

1.   Pulpit Commentary, Scholar John Gill (James, Chapter 3.)

2.   Andrew Newberg and Mark Robert Waldman, *Words Can Change Your Brain* (New York, NY: Plume, 2013), 34

Conclusion

1.   Charles Spurgeon, *Holy Spirit Power* (New Kensignton, PA: Whitaker House, 1996), 55

2.   Matthew Henry's Commentary on the Whole Bible – Logos Bible Software (Matthew, Chapter 6.)

3.   Mandisa's blog post about her decision of not attending the Grammy ceremony: http://mandisaofficial.com/home/i-missed-the-grammy-awards-and-i-won/